VOYAGES

STORIES OF AMERICA AND THE SEA

A companion to the exhibition at Mystic Seaport

Andrew W. German

Mystic Seaport
The Museum of America and the Sea

Mystic, Connecticut

Mystic Seaport Museum, Inc., Mystic, CT 06355-0990
© 2000 by Mystic Seaport Museum, Inc.
All rights reserved
First edition
Printed in Hong Kong

Cataloging-in-Publication Data

German, Andrew W., 1950-
        Voyages : stories of America and the sea / Andrew W. German.
— 1st ed. — Mystic, Conn. : Mystic Seaport Museum, c2000.
        p. : ill. ; cm.
        "A companion volume to the exhibition at Mystic Seaport."
        Bibliography : p.
        Includes index.

        1. United States - History. 2. United States - Emigration and
immigration - History. 3. United States - History, Naval. 4. United
States - Commerce - History. 5. Fisheries - United States - History.
6. Boats and boating - United States - History. 7. Sea in art.

E183.9.G47
ISBN 0-913372-91-9

Designed by Trish Sinsigalli LaPointe, Old Mystic, Connecticut

Extract from "The Negro Speaks of Rivers," from COLLECTED POEMS
by Langston Hughes. Copyright © 1994 by the Estate of Langston Hughes.
Reprinted by permission of Alfred A. Knopf, a division of Random House Inc.

CONTENTS

FOREWORD

As the seventh decade of Mystic Seaport's service to the nation began in the early 1990s, the staff and the Trustees began a process of self-examination, evaluation, and planning. We looked at the Museum's many successes in preservation and education over the years, and we looked back at the goals expressed by the visionaries who founded the Museum in 1929. When we examined the offerings of other maritime museums we realized that no museum in the country was introducing its visitors to the full sweep of the American maritime story. Although Mystic Seaport has long been known as a museum of nineteenth-century New England, due to the prominence of our outdoor exhibits and ships, we knew that our library, our publications, and particularly our academic programs at the undergraduate and graduate levels had long been representing the national story. Examining our collections, our exhibition potential, and our future opportunities to use emerging technologies, we concluded that we could make a significant contribution as the Museum of America and the Sea.

The concept is compelling. The maritime story represents the development of this nation in dramatic form, and the themes of human beings living, working, and playing on the sea in so many ways represent the full range of our heroic and creative potential. And, although the sea is a foreign place to most of us, we feel its influence daily in such basic ways as our access to goods from around the world, our use of marine resources, and our choice of water sports. We came to believe strongly that it should be our mission to make this relationship clear, both at the Museum itself and through our outreach efforts.

The Museum's Board of Trustees approved this vision in 1994, and the staff set about making progress toward this objective immediately. The curators assessed the Museum's holdings and identified areas that needed to be enhanced to fulfill this refocused and expanded mission. With the assistance of the National Endowment for the Humanities we created two permanently endowed positions for America and the Sea Research Fellows, one of whom, Andrew German, is the author of this book. And most importantly, we enlisted the faculty of our graduate-level academic program, the Munson Institute, and Andy German, to write the "magnum opus" *America and the Sea: A Maritime History*. This hefty volume has received excellent reviews internationally and serves as the foundation for many of the other manifestations of America and the Sea at Mystic Seaport.

For any museum, an exhibition is the obvious manifestation of the institution's mission. For Mystic Seaport that signature exhibition is *Voyages: Stories of America and the Sea*. We knew we could not convey the breadth and depth of the story of America and the Sea in a single exhibit. Our goal should be to introduce visitors from around the country and around the globe to essential themes in the nation's ongoing relationship with the sea around it. After much discussion we agreed on seven broad themes reflecting this relationship: the sea as a highway of economic and cultural exchange, as a place of essential natural resources, as a common ground of international conflict and cooperation, as an impetus to technological development, as a place of recreation, as an inspiration for creative expression and personal development, and as an influence on human communities at sea as well as along its shores.

With support from the Connecticut Humanities Concil, and under the steady guidance of Director of Exhibitions Stuart Parnes, working with a team of staff members, the concept for the exhibition emerged. It called for exploring America and the Sea through seven sections derived from these themes, each of which would incorporate both past and present stories to convey the extent of this maritime adventure. In the exhibit, three sections look at the sea as an avenue of connection. The initial section focuses on the flow of humanity who immigrated by sea to create the diversity of this nation. Another addresses coastal and river traffic as the lifeblood of the nation, while the third looks at America's relationship to international ocean trade. Other sections emphasize the U.S. Navy's role on the common ground of the sea, the development of recreation on and along the water, our use of the sea's many resources, and ways that the sea inspires our creative impulses.

Clearly and appropriately, the exhibition, *Voyages*, is not an attempt to convert the book, *America and the Sea: A Maritime History*, into an exhibit. Different techniques are used in each medium, and each medium is an effective way of reaching certain audiences. We expected that many visitors to the Museum and to *Voyages* would want a way to "take the exhibition with them" in the form of a compact exhibit companion book. Therefore, Andy German, who had been such a strong contributor to the earlier book and the exhibition development, undertook to shape the textual content and combine it with images from *Voyages: Stories of America and the Sea* to produce this volume.

During the creation of this exhibition and book, the Museum continued to develop other ways of presenting the stories of America and the Sea. Looking to the future, we made a major commitment to digitize significant portions of our library and other collections in order to be able to provide researchers and scholars around the world with electronic access to materials that relate to the story of America and the Sea. A grant from the National Endowment for the Humanities supported the beginning of our effort to develop an on-line exhibition to be called *Making Connections with America and the Sea* in collaboration with twenty-two sister institutions and scholars. Mystic Seaport also continues to explore ways to bring the stories of America and the Sea to the public through a variety of media, from books and magazines to radio, CD-ROM, and television.

All of this is challenging and exciting for everyone involved with Mystic Seaport. Through *Voyages: Stories of America and the Sea* and our future efforts, we will accomplish our mission of creating a broad public understanding of the relationship of America and the Sea

J. REVELL CARR
President and Director
Mystic Seaport Museum, Inc.

Part One

COMING TO AMERICA

Do you know how your ancestors came to America? Unless they were Native Americans, the answer is most likely "on a ship."

The sea voyage to America was an exciting, frightening, unforgettable experience, shared by immigrants from Europe, South America, Africa, and Asia. Some travelers were brutally forced to these shores as slaves. A fortunate few crossed in comfortable staterooms. Most huddled together in overcrowded sailing or steamships. All faced the unpredictable challenges of the sea crossing, and some did not survive.

The first settlers in North America walked across a land bridge to Alaska during the Ice Age. More than 10,000 years later, their descendants were there to meet the European "discoverers" who came by sea and began a new era of settlement. For 350 years, the greatest human migration in history progressed across the world's oceans to settle the North American continent. Beginning in the early 1600s, European colonists began to settle permanently on the wild coast of North America. These pioneers endured the uncertainty, exposure, and privation of a long sea passage before their arrival in an unfamiliar land. Some came for a more fruitful life; other well-known groups, such as the Pilgrims, Puritans, and Quakers, came to practice their religion without the persecution they faced at home. Most of them came from the land and were bound to the land, enduring a disorienting ordeal at sea.

"A ship at sea may well be compared to a cradle rocked by a careful mother's hand. . . So a ship may often be rocked too and again upon the troublesome sea, yet seldom doth it sink or overturn because it is kept by that careful hand of Providence by which it is rocked," suggested William Wood in his 1634 pamphlet *New Englands Prospect*, encouraging travelers that their health might actually improve at sea. More likely was the experience of Gabriel Archer, on a passage to Virginia in 1609: "many of our men fell sick of the Calenture [a tropical fever], and out of two of our ships was throwne over-boord thirtie two persons. . . but in the *Blessing* we had not any sicke, albeit we had twenty women and children." Then, for 44 hours, "there hapned a most terrible and vehement storme, which was the taile of the West Indian Horacano; this tempest separated all our Fleet one from another, and it was so violent that men could scarce stand upon Deckes, neither could any man heare another speake."

Illustration on page 6: Millions of Europeans endured a transatlantic passage to seek a new life in America. Grand steamships like the 700-foot North German Lloyd Line *Kronprinzessin Cecilie* of 1907 had basic living accommodations for many hundreds in lower-deck steerage compartments. (Mystic Seaport, 96.142.17; Claire White-Peterson photo)

Until the American Revolution, a large number of English immigrants were indentured servants, who bound themselves for a number of years to a master in America to pay for their passage. William Moraley sailed to Philadelphia as an indentured servant, describing his experience in his 1743 book, *The Unfortunate.*

Every Adventurer had his Apparel given him for the Voyage, which was, a Sea Jacket, two coarse chequ'd Shirts, a Woollen Waistcoat, two coarse Handkerchiefs, one Pair of Hose, a Woollen Cap, and a pair of bad new Shoes. . . . Three Biscuits were given to each Man for the Day, and a small Piece of Salt Beef, no bigger then a Penny Chop of Mutton. Some Days we had Stockfish, when every Man was obliged to beat his Share with a Maul to make it tender, with a little stinking Butter for Sauce.

Every Morning and Evening the Captain called every one of us to the Cabbin Door, where we received a Thimble full of bad Brandy. We were obliged to turn out every four Hours, with the Sailors, to watch; which was to prevent our falling sick, by herding under Deck. . . .

We attempted to drink the Salt Water, but it increased our Thirst. Sometimes, but rarely, it rained, when we set our Hats upon Deck to catch the Water; but it sliding down the Sails, gave it the Taste of Tarr.

Africans first arrived in the English colonies in 1619. By the 1680s Southern agriculture began to depend on African slaves rather than indentured servants for labor. For 130 years, a legal slave trade procured Africans through kidnapping or war, delivered them to ports along a 3,000-mile stretch of West African coast, and shipped them under horrific conditions.

Olaudah Equiano was born at Essaka, Benin (now eastern Nigeria), in 1745, the son of an Igbo embrenche or chief. When he was eleven, Equiano and his sister were kidnapped and sold into slavery in Africa. Soon they were sold again and separated. Eventually Equiano was taken to the coast, as he described in his 1789 book, *The Interesting Narrative of the Life of Olaudah Equiano, or Gustavus Vassa, the African.*

The first object that saluted my eyes when I arrived on the coast was the sea, and a slave ship, which was then riding at anchor, and waiting for its cargo. . . . I was immediately handled and tossed up to see if I was sound, by some of the crew; and I was now persuaded that I had got into a world of bad spirits, and that they were going to kill me. Their complexions too, differing so much from ours, their long hair, and the language they spoke, which

1654, first Jews settle in New York

1682, Welsh Quakers settle in new colony of Pennsylvania

1683, German Quakers arrive in Pennsylvania

1685, French Hugenots settle in North America

1689, Scottish and Irish emigration begins

1690, beginning of large-scale African slave trade to North America totaling more than 660,000 before 1808

For 250 years, emigrants to America braved the ocean under sail. By the 1850s, large wooden ships like the *International*, sometimes sailing on schedule as packets, were transporting an increasing flow of Europeans to America. In 1853, 425 Mormon immigrants made a 54-day passage from Liverpool to New Orleans aboard the *International*. Oil painting by William York, 1861. (Mystic Seaport, 67.75)

Willing immigrants faced hardships enough at sea. Like this child, more than 9,000,000 Africans, sold into slavery and shipped across the Atlantic against their will, endured inhuman conditions of the Middle Passage between 1500 and 1870. More than 660,000 of these captive Africans were brought to what are now the United States.(Mystic Seaport, G.W. Blunt White Library, *Illustrated London News*, 20 June 1857)

was very different from any I had ever heard, united to confirm me in this belief. When I looked round the ship too, and saw a large furnace or copper boiling and a multitude of black people, of every description, chained together, every one of their countenances expressing dejection and sorrow, I no longer doubted of my fate; and, quite overpowered with horror and anguish, I fell motionless on the deck, and fainted. . . .

I was soon put down under the decks, and there I received such a salutation in my nostrils as I had never experienced in my life: so that, with the loathsomeness of the stench, and with my crying together, I became so sick and low that I was not able to eat, nor had I the least desire to taste any thing. I now wished for the last friend, death, to relieve me. . . .

The stench of the hold, while we were on the coast, was so intolerably loathsome, that it was dangerous to remain there for any time, and some of us had been permitted to stay on the deck for the fresh air; but now that the whole ship's cargo were confined together, it became absolutely pestilential. The closeness of the place, and the heat of the climate, added to the number in the ship, being so crowded that each had scarcely room to turn himself, almost suffocated us. This produced copious perspiration, so that the air soon became unfit for respiration, from a variety of loathsome

9

☞ *Congo Slaves.*—The Sale of the Port Mary's Cargo of 360 very prime SLAVES, will commence *THIS DAY*, the 20th instant, at ten o'clock, on board, at Gadsden's Wharf.

WM. BOYD.

June 19.

☞ *Prime Mandingo Negroes.*—The Sale of the Cargo of the Ship *Hibernia*, Capt. PRATT, from Cape Mount, consisting of 217 Prime MANDINGO SLAVES, will commence on board, at Gadsden's Wharf, *THIS MORNING*, the 14th inst. at 10 o'clock

HENRY & JOHN KER.

June 14.

☞ *Prime Africans for Sale.*—The ale of the Ship CERES's cargo of 300 Prime, Healthy NEGROES, will commence on board at Gadsden's Wharf, THIS DAY, the 27th instant. Apply to

GIBSON & BROADFOOT.

May 27.

Until the transatlantic slave trade to the U.S. was prohibited by federal law after 1 January 1808, more than 660,000 Africans were legally wrenched from their families and native cultures to be sold in North America for a life of slave labor. On 28 July 1806 the *Charleston Courier* advertised the sales of nearly 1,000 newly arrived Africans, including these two groups identified only by their places of origin. (Mystic Seaport, G.W. Blunt White Library)

Detail of steerage accommodations for Irish immigrants. (Mystic Seaport, G.W. Blunt White Library, *Illustrated London News*, 10 May 1851)

smells, and brought on a sickness among the slaves, of which many died, thus falling victims to the improvident avarice, as I may call it, of their purchasers. This deplorable situation was again aggravated by the galling of the chains, now become insupportable; and the filth of necessary tubs, into which the children often fell, and were almost suffocated. The shrieks of the women, and the groans of the dying, rendered it a scene of horror almost inconceivable, . . . and I began to hope that death would soon put an end to my miseries. . . .

One day, when we had a smooth sea and moderate wind, two of my wearied countrymen, who were chained together, (I was near them at the time) preferring death to such a life of misery, somehow made through the nettings and jumped into the sea: immediately another quite dejected fellow, who on account of his illness was suffered to be out of irons also followed their example; and I believe many more would very soon have done the same, if they had not been prevented by the ship's crew. . . .

At least 15 percent of these passengers died during the terrible "Middle Passage" across the Atlantic, some during revolts, most from disease and despair. Estimates vary, but at least 660,000 unwilling Africans were landed in North America before the end of the legal slave trade in 1808, and 50,000 more may have arrived before U.S. slavery was ended as a result of the Civil War.

After 1820 the pace of immigration increased. Between 1820 and 1950, more than 39 million people came to settle in the United States, most of them by sea. Helen Hunt Jackson's poem "Emigravit," ca. 1880, suggests the parting.

> *With sails full set, the ship her anchor weighs.*
> *Strange names shine out beneath her figure-head.*
> *What glad farewells with eager eyes are said!*
> *What cheer for him who goes, and him who stays!*
> *Fair skies, rich lands, new homes, and untried days*
> *Some go to seek: the rest but wait instead,*
> *Watching the way wherein their comrades led,*
> *Until the next staunch ship her flag doth raise.*
> *Who knows what myriad colonies there are*
> *Of fairest fields, and rich, undreamed-of gains*

ca. 1840, beginnings of Cape Verdean immigration as a consequence of employment in New England whaling industry

1840-90, like other religious pilgrims before them, 90,000 Mormon converts cross the ocean to gather at their zion in Utah

Detail of steerage accommodations for Irish immigrants. (Mystic Seaport, G.W. Blunt White Library, *Illustrated London News*, 10 May 1851)

1842, annual immigration first exceeds 100,000

1849, annual immigration first exceeds 250,000

1854, Chinese laborers begin arriving in significant numbers, most intending to return to China after accumulating wealth

U.S. first establishes relations with Japan

1855, Castle Garden at New York established as principal East Coast immigrant processing depot, operating until 1890

ca. 1880, Baltimore becomes second leading destination for transatlantic immigrants

An immigrant register documents the names, ages, origins, and occupations of more than 600 men, women, and children who emigrated from Liverpool to the U.S. aboard the ship *Western Empire* in 1853. (Mystic Seaport, G.W. Blunt White Library, Collection 152, box 54, folder 10)

1881, annual immigration first exceeds 500,000

1882, U.S. establishes commercial relations with Korea

Chinese Exclusion Act limits entry of Chinese laborers

Opened in 1892, the federal immigration depot at Ellis Island in New York Harbor processed 12,000,000 immigrants during its 62 years of operation. (Mystic Seaport, 85.74.1)

ca. 1885, increase in immigration from Russia, Poland, Italy, and Eastern Europe

1891, Japanese immigration begins

1892, Ellis Island opens as principal East Coast immigrant processing station

1898, U.S. annexes Hawaii; Spain cedes the Philippines, Guam, and Puerto Rico to the U.S. to settle Spanish-American War

Immigrant at Ellis Island, 1924. (Negative 19684F, © Mystic Seaport, Inc., Rosenfeld Collection)

Thick planted in the distant shining plains
Which we call sky because they lie so far?
Oh, write of me, not "Died in bitter pains,"
But "Emigrated to another star!"

In his 1849 novel *Redburn*, Herman Melville conjured a graphic appreciation of the immigrant's ordeal at sea.

To provide for their wants, a far larger supply of water was needed than upon the outward-bound passage. Accordingly, besides the usual number of casks on deck, rows of immense tierces were lashed amid-ships, all along the between-decks, forming a sort of aisle on each side, furnishing access to four rows of bunks,—three tiers, one above another,—against the ship's sides; two tiers being placed over the tierces of water in the middle. These bunks were rapidly knocked together with coarse planks. They looked more like dog-kennels than any thing else; especially as the place was so gloomy and dark; no light coming down except through the fore and after hatchways, both of which were covered with little houses called "booby-hatches." Upon the main-hatches, which were well calked and covered over with heavy tarpaulins, the "passengers'-galley" was solidly lashed down.

This galley was a large open stove, or iron range—made expressly for emigrant ships, wholly unprotected from the weather, and where alone the emigrants are permitted to cook their food while at sea. . . .

The wind was fair; the weather mild; the sea most smooth; and the poor emigrants were in high spirits at so auspicious a beginning of their voyage. They were reclining all over the decks, talking of soon seeing America, and relating how the agent had told them, that twenty days would be an uncommonly long voyage.

[T]hough the English authorities have imposed a law, providing that every captain of an emigrant ship bound for any port of America shall see to it, that each passenger is provided with rations of food for sixty days; yet, all this has not deterred mercenary shipmasters and unprincipled agents from practicing the grossest deception; nor exempted the emigrants themselves from the very sufferings intended to be averted. . . .

How, then, with the friendless emigrants, stowed away like bales of cotton, and packed like slaves in a slave-ship; confined in a place that, during storm time, must be closed against both light and air. . . .

We had not been at sea one week, when to hold your head down the fore hatchway was like holding it down a suddenly opened cess-pool. . . .

12

Immigrants arrived in America with few possessions from their former lives. Anna M. Rafsbach used this chest when she came to Baltimore aboard the North German Lloyd Line steamship *Hohenzollern* around 1880. (Mystic Seaport, 99.187)

1900-07, "Gentlemen's Agreements" restrict Japanese immigration

1900-20, Austrian-Hungarian, Italian, and Russian immigrants predominate

1905, annual immigration first exceeds 1,000,000; one of six times, 1905-1914, that more than a million immigrants arrive

1907, peak immigration year: 1,285,349 persons arrive

By 1900, immigrants coming to America carried these health inspection cards (Mystic Seaport, G.W. Blunt White Library, VFM 1891, VFM 1868)

The sight that greeted us, upon entering, was wretched indeed. It was like entering a crowded jail. From the rows of rude bunks, hundreds of meager, begrimed faces were turned upon us; while seated upon the chests, were scores of unshaven men, smoking tea-leaves, and creating a suffocating vapor. But this vapor was better than the native air of the place, which from almost unbelievable causes, was foetid in the extreme. In every corner, the females were huddled together, weeping and lamenting; children were asking bread from their mothers, who had none to give; and old men, seated upon the floor, were leaning back against the heads of the water-casks, with closed eyes and fetching their breath with a gasp. . . .

On the sixth morning, the weather merged into a gale, to which we stripped our ship to a storm-stay-sail. In ten hours' time, the waves ran in mountains; and the Highlander rose and fell like some vast buoy on the water. Shrieks and lamentations were driven to leeward, and drowned in the roar of the wind among the cordage; while we gave to the gale the blackened bodies of five more of the dead.

But as the dying departed, the places of two of them were filled in the rolls of humanity, by the birth of two infants, whom the plague, panic, and gale had hurried into the world before their time. The first cry of one of these infants, was almost simultaneous with the splash of its father's body in the sea. Thus we come and we go. But, surrounded by death, both mothers and babes survived.

How, then, with these emigrants, who, three thousand miles from home, suddenly found themselves deprived of brothers and husbands, with but a few pounds, or perhaps but a few shillings, to buy food in a strange land?

1910, Angel Island opens as Asian immigrant processing center at San Francisco

1924, National Origins Act establishes quotas and severely restricts immigration

1940, Angel Island closes

After a long transpacific passage, these Asian men prepare to disembark and pass through the Angel Island immigration station in San Francisco Bay, which operated as a hospital and detention center from 1910 to 1940. After the Chinese Exclusion Act of 1882 and the "Gentlemen's Agreements" of 1900-07, Asian entry into the U.S. was strictly limited. Not until 1943 were Chinese immigrants welcomed, and not until 1952 could Asians become U.S. citizens. (90-G-124-519, courtesy National Archives)

1945, immigration of "displaced persons" permitted in aftermath of World War II

1954, Ellis Island closes after processing 12,000,000 immigrants during 62 years of operation

ca. 1960, air transportation supersedes sea travel for most immigrants

1965, Immigration Act abolishes national quotas among immigrants

Camarioca "boat lift" brings Cuban refugees to U.S. by water

As the human tide increased, the passage became somewhat easier, with larger, faster vessels and regulations requiring ships to meet basic standards for the nutrition and accommodation of immigrants. Many sailing ships had carried immigrants when other cargo was unavailable, but transatlantic steamship lines began to treat immigrants as standard westbound cargo. The increasingly large steamships, which grew from 300 feet in the 1870s to nearly 1,000 feet with vessels like the *Titanic* by 1910, included basic third-class steerage accommodations for hundreds. Lines like the North German Lloyd, Hamburg American, Cunard, or Red Star provided inexpensive travel across Europe to ports of departure, and provided basic food and sanitary conditions on board ship as required by law.

By the time a new immigrant processing facility was opened on Ellis Island in New York Harbor in 1892, immigration was an orderly process. Some passengers—usually young males—were pioneers setting forth to establish themselves in America. More were women, children, and elderly coming as part of a chain migration to join husbands or sons who had preceded them.

As political, economic, or social upheaval afflicted their home nations, various ethnic or national groups predominated in the ocean trek: Irish and Germans from the 1820s through the 1850s, and Austrians, Italians, and Russians from 1900 through the 1920s, when annual quota restrictions were placed on immigration.

As a crowd greets the American transatlantic liner *St. Paul* at New York in 1903, first- and second-class passengers prepare to disembark and pass through customs. As many as 500 immigrants in steerage on the lower decks will be ferried to Ellis Island, on the horizon above the lifeboat, for inspection before entering America. (Negative B379, © Mystic Seaport, Inc., Rosenfeld Collection)

14

Until immigration quotas were imposed by the National Origins Act of 1924, as many as a million immigrants entered America annually. After 1892 the majority of them came through Ellis Island, like these new arrivals in 1924 who have survived an ocean crossing and now wait to make travel connections either to join family or to pioneer a new life in their new land. (Negative 19684F, © Mystic Seaport, Inc., Rosenfeld Collection)

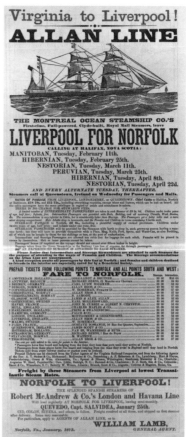

Eight-year-old Paulina Caramando came from Naples on board the *Dante Alighieri* in 1920. "The first-class people, all the rich people, were way above. I'd look up at them, they were all dressed nice, and we were like a flock of sheep down below."

On the West Coast, Asian migration was different in intent. The Chinese, who first came to California around 1850 during the gold rush, viewed America as the "Gold Mountain." Young Chinese men came to work and earn a fortune before returning to their families in China, although the realities of life in America meant that few earned enough to make the return passage. By the 1890s young Japanese men were coming to Hawai'i and the West Coast for agricultural work, also intending to return home with enough money to marry.

In August of 1897 I went to the U.S. by cargo boat, Yamaguchi Maru *from Kobe. I was then 16. The third class accommodations were crowded with more than 160 passengers and there wasn't any bunk in which to rest. I slept spreading my own mat and blanket on the wooden floor in the front hatch where there were no windows and no lights. . . . The hatch was tightly closed and there was no circulation of air, so we were all tortured by the bad odor. As the boat was small, whenever a high wave hit us the top deck was submerged and the sound of the screw [propeller] grinding in empty*

Transatlantic immigration became an orderly flow with the advent of scheduled steamship lines. This 1873 poster announces economical Allen Line service between Liverpool and Norfolk, Virginia, for Europeans wishing to resettle in the American heartland. (Mystic Seaport, 97.13.1)

1972, first Haitian "boat people" arrive in Florida

1980, Mariel boat lift brings additional Cubans by sea

1980-94, thousands of Haitians seek refuge in U.S. by sea

1994, "last wave" of seaborne immigrants arrive from Cuba

15

Although they came intending only to work until they earned enough to return home and prosper in their native lands, Asian immigrants faced increasing restrictions on entry into the U.S. (Mystic Seaport, G.W. Blunt White Library, *Harper's Weekly*, 20 May 1876)

space chilled us. The food was second class Nankin rice and salted-kelp, with dirty clams preserved by boiling in soy sauce. . . . I shivered, thinking that I would probably go back to Japan some years later in just such a boat.

Recollections of Chojiro Kubo, quoted in Kazuo Ito, *Issei: A History of Japanese Immigrants in North America* (Seattle: Japanese Community Service, 1973), 32.

Because of strong recial prejudice in the U.S., Chinese and Japanese alike faced restrictions upon entering the U.S., and harsh discrimination wherever they settled. Some left their stories in the form of poetry on the walls of the detention center on Angel Island in San Francisco Bay.

> *. . . . It was on the day that the Weaver Maiden*
> *met the Cowherd*
> *That I took passage on the President Lincoln.*
> *I ate wind and tasted waves for more than*
> *twenty days.*
> *Fortunately, I arrived safely on the American*
> *continent*
> *I thought I could land in a few days.*
> *How was I to know I would become a*
> *prisoner suffering in the wooden building?*
> *The barbarians' abuse is really difficult to*
> *take. . . .*

16

The nature of immigration by sea changed after World War II. Hundreds of thousands fled Europe in the first years after the war, but the flow declined so much that the Ellis Island facility was closed in 1954. At the same time, transatlantic travel was shifting from ship to airplane. In 1957, for the first time, more people crossed the Atlantic by air than by sea, and by 1970 few transatlantic passenger ships remained in operation.

But sea immigration did not end; it merely became more desperate. Economic and political upheaval in the Caribbean since the 1950s, particularly the revolution in Cuba and the dictatorship in Haiti, resulted in waves of refugees fleeing Haiti and Cuba for the U.S. by boat. In desperation, they boarded anything that floated, and many were lost in the turbulent waters of the Florida Straits. Between the authorized Cuban "boat lifts" and the escape of others under the cover of darkness, several hundred thousand Cubans made the 90-mile crossing to Florida. During the same period, many thousands of Haitians set sail in small boats for the 600-mile passage to America.

Although the great seaborne flow of individuals who endured the ordeal of an ocean passage to populate this nation has ended, recent stowaways on cargo ships and vessel-loads of Chinese still represent the spirit that sustained earlier generations during the ocean trials that brought them to a new beginning in America.

After 35 years as a Cuban fishing boat, the 25-foot *Analuisa* became a refugee boat in 1994, carrying 19 people toward a new life in Florida. After her occupants were rescued by a cruise ship, the *Analuisa* was boarded by another group of six to complete their passage to freedom. (Mystic Seaport, 94.130; Judy Beisler photo)

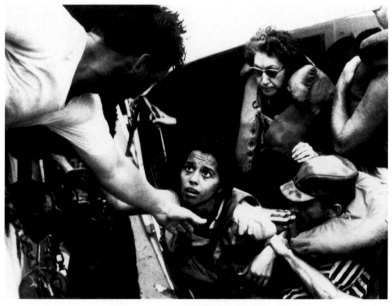

Beginning with the Camarioca "boat lift" of 1965, the last wave of sea-borne immigration into the U.S. has come from Cuba and Haiti, where economic and political conditions compelled tens of thousands to embark in small boats for a better life in America. (26-G-10-13-65, courtesy National Archives)

Part Two

FOLLOWING THE RIVERS

Since the days of the earliest Native settlements, coastal and inland waterways have connected Americans to one another. On board countless canoes, boats, and ships we loaded our possessions, families, traditions, and dreams. Rivers, lakes, canals, and coastal waters carried them all from harbor to harbor and deep into the nation's heartland.

Of all the vast system of waterways, it is our great rivers that have touched the lives of most Americans. Even today, in an age of railways, interstate highways, and air travel, the lifeblood of the United States remains its rivers. Muddy brown or clear blue, the steady flow of America's rivers continues to draw us near and pull us along.

The Europeans who came to North America in the seventeenth century learned what the Native Americans had long known: water was the easiest way to travel around the continent. Indeed, waterways—both coastal and inland—were the nation's first "interstate highways."

As soon as European settlers established ports, from Boston and New York to Charleston, these communities became the focal points of coastal transportation, receiving raw materials from their nearby hinterlands by water and sending back manufactured or imported goods, as well as information or ideas. Water transportation also connected the major ports, carrying passengers and exchanging regional commodities and communication.

Among the early acts of the new federal government in 1789 was a tariff on foreign vessels engaged in trade between American ports, and this trade was completely prohibited by the Navigation Act of 1817. This cabotage act (reserving the coastal trade to U.S. vessels) protected the U.S. coastal fleet from foreign competition. Even when the U.S. fleet engaged in overseas trade was at its height, the coastal fleet was far larger.

After the U.S. seized California and settled the upper Pacific region, trade between the East and West Coasts was protected, even though it required a 13,000-mile passage round Cape Horn. Many large American sailing ships in competitive foreign trade increased their business by making a run to California as part of their global trading.

19

**Navigating the Nation's
Waterways: A Chronology**

ca. 1,000, Native Americans use
major North American rivers as
trade routes

1614, establishment of Dutch Ft.
Oranje near present site of
Albany, New York, opens Hudson
River to European trade

1673, Jacques Marquette and
Louis Jolliet travel across the
Great Lakes and explore the
upper portion of the Mississippi
River

ca. 1680-ca. 1850, "Voyageurs"
use the lake and river networks
for fur trapping and trade with
American Indians

1682, Robert Cavelier, Sieur
de La Salle, travels down the
Mississippi to its mouth and
claims the region for France

1701, French establish outpost
at the site of Detroit

1718, French establish settlement
of New Orleans

1764, French establish outpost at
the site of St. Louis

Illustration on page 18: This
1855 map of the United States
emphasized the nation's essential
maritime connections. (Mystic
Seaport, G.W. Blunt White
Library)

Sailing vessels predominated in the coastal fleet until almost 1900, but steam power represented the true revolution in coastal trade during the 1800s. Robert Fulton's *North River Steam Boat* proved that a commercial steamboat would work when it ran up the Hudson River in 1807. Soon, inventors and investors were building more efficient steamboats and establishing new lines. However, Fulton and his backers had obtained a monopoly on steamboat operation in New York waters. Not until the U.S. Supreme Court ruled, in the 1824 case *Gibbons v. Ogden*, that federal regulation of interstate commerce took precedence over state restrictions did coastal steamboats run freely into New York, the nation's leading port. Soon, large coastal steamboats were providing express mail and passenger service between the large ports while smaller boats shuttled back and forth in the hinterlands.

The great river network of America's heartland spans two-thirds of the continent, from western Pennsylvania and eastern Tennessee to Minnesota, Montana, and Oklahoma, draining into the sea through Louisiana's Mississippi River Delta. Native Americans had used the inland waters for thousands of years before Jacques Marquette and Louis Jolliet became the first Europeans to explore the Mississippi. After René-Robert Cavelier, Sieur de La Salle, claimed the Mississippi for France in 1682, France established outposts at the sites of Pittsburgh, St. Louis, and New Orleans. Pittsburgh and the Ohio River Valley became part of the United States in the Treaty of Paris that ended the American Revolution, while President Thomas Jefferson obtained the Mississippi River Valley from France with the Louisiana Purchase in 1803.

The rivers became integral to the settlement of the west. Leaving St. Louis, Lewis and Clark followed the Missouri River west to Montana, then crossed the continental divide in the Rocky Mountains and continued down the Snake and Columbia Rivers to the sea. Settlers would later follow these watercourses as they traveled west.

When the Louisiana Purchase unplugged the mouth of the Mississippi to U.S. trade, the Ohio-Mississippi River system became the artery of trade between the Midwest and East. Rough flatboats carried produce downriver to New Orleans while more maneuverable keelboats could travel both ways on the river, however slowly. The free-spirited boatmen became legendary for their bravery and brawling. Mike Fink, "half horse and half alligator," came to symbolize the rivermen, even after

20

Americans' impressions of the Mississippi River as a transportation artery were largely shaped by popular prints like this 1860 Currier & Ives lithograph, *A Midnight Race on the Mississippi*. It depicts a race between the 1849 steamboat *Eclipse* and the *Natchez* of 1854, fast boats that provided mail and passenger service on the lower Mississippi. The artist, Frances F. Palmer, an Englishwoman who worked as a lithographer after immigrating, worked from a sketch of the *Natchez* because she had never seen the Mississippi River. (Mystic Seaport, 96.126)

1790, Captain Robert Gray locates mouth of the Columbia River

1790-1840, era of flatboats for carrying cargo downstream on the Ohio and Mississippi Rivers, and keelboats for travel in both directions

1803, Louisiana Purchase opens Mississippi River to U.S. trade

1803-06, Lewis and Clark Expedition follows Missouri and Columbia River systems to explore the U.S. western territories acquired through the Louisiana Purchase

1807, Robert Fulton's *North River Steam Boat* carries passengers up the Hudson River from New York City to Albany, inaugurating commercial steamboat service in the U.S.

1811, steamboat *New Orleans* travels down Ohio and Mississippi Rivers from Pittsburgh to New Orleans, inaugurating steamboat service on the western rivers

1815, beginning of steamboat service on Long Island Sound

Between 1825 and 1850, Americans in many states dug artificial rivers to link communities and provide economical transportation routes to deliver their products to larger markets. Carrying both passengers and goods, these canals offered easy access to the west, expanding settlement and extending the national economy in the years before the railroad. (Mystic Seaport, G.W. Blunt White Library)

faster, more efficient steamboats made them obsolete by the time of the Civil War.

The steamboat arrived on the rivers in 1811 when the *New Orleans* traveled downstream from Pittsburgh to New Orleans. After the upstream passage of the *Enterprise* in 1815, the steamboat began to dominate the rivers, shortening the 100-day round trip between New Orleans and Pittsburgh to just 30 days and greatly reducing freight rates. By about 1830 the western steamboat had taken its classic form, with wide, shallow hull, tall smokestacks, several spindly decks with the pilothouse perched on top, and side wheels or a stern wheel to drive the boat. With hundreds of these boats navigating the looping rivers, the river ports of Pittsburgh, Cincinnati, St. Louis, and New Orleans became some of America's most important cities. River steamboats became essential in moving people, in carrying cotton and other produce of the Southern agricultural economy to market, in delivering goods and information to remote landings all along the rivers, in delivering immigrants to the interior, and in employing many thousands of men and women, from skilled pilots to unskilled roustabouts.

But river transportation remained hazardous. High-pressure boilers exploded all too often, and shifting sandbars,

The 161-foot stern-wheel steamboat *Bertrand*, built at Wheeling, West Virginia, in 1864, represents the variety of western rivers steamboat used on the Missouri River. These boats might travel 2,000 miles upstream from St. Louis to the head of navigation at Fort Benton, Montana, delivering goods to the mining communities. To negotiate the shallow, twisting Missouri, the boats had extremely shallow hulls and stern wheels. The "grasshopper leg" spars at the bow were used to lever the boat over sandbars in the river. On her first passage upstream, the *Bertrand* struck a submerged "snag" (log) and sank north of Omaha, Nebraska, in April 1865. More than a hundred years later the remains were recovered in a field far from the modern river course. The cargo preserved on board reveals much about the trading patterns that supplied the western communities. (Mystic Seaport, 98.88.1; Claire White-Peterson photo)

The busy St. Louis waterfront harbored hundreds of steamboats, which provided regular service up the Missouri River, up and down the Mississippi, and up the Ohio River in a transportation web that stretched north and south from St. Paul to New Orleans, and east and west from Pittsburgh, Pennsylvania, to Fort Benton, Montana. On the strength of its commerce and the flow of immigrant settlers arriving by river, St. Louis became one of the leading American cities in the mid-1800s. (Mystic Seaport, 94.111.8)

"snags" (floating logs), and submerged stumps sank many steamers each year. With his local knowledge and his ability to "read" river conditions, the pilot was the most important person on a steamboat. In his 1874 book, *Life on the Mississippi,* the former steamboat pilot Samuel Clemens—Mark Twain—suggested the art of piloting when he described how a Mississippi River pilot might approach a difficult stretch of river, such as Plum Point, 100 miles below Cairo, Illinois:

"It was in the night, there, and I ran it the way one of the boys on the Diana *told me; started out about fifty yards above the wood-pile on the false point, and held on the cabin under Plum Point till I raised the reef—quarter less twain [a quarter fathom less than two fathoms, or 10 1/2 feet deep]—then straightened up for the middle bar till I got well abreast the old one-limbed cottonwood in the bend, then got my stern on the cottonwood, and head on the low place above the point, and came through a-booming—nine and a half."*

After the American Revolution engineers looked to the English canal system and began to explore ways of creating artificial rivers to extend efficient transportation into developing areas of America. Despite these early efforts the "canal era" did not begin until New York State financed construction of the Erie Canal between 1817 and 1825. This 325-mile trench, connecting the Hudson River with Lake Erie, created an efficient water route from New York to the West.

By funneling western grain to the sea, making New York an entrepôt for the upper Midwest, and carrying European immigrants west to settle, the Erie Canal increased the importance of New York. Other ports quickly planned similar canals to tap near and distant hinterlands. During the following 20 years, major canal networks were dug across Pennsylvania, through Ohio, and as far west as Illinois. Several, including the Schuylkill, Delaware and Hudson, and Chesapeake and Ohio, were primarily coal carriers, delivering this important energy source to the seaboard. Others, like the Erie, were more general cargo and passenger routes. The nation's longest was Indiana's Wabash and Erie, which stretched 458 miles when it was completed in 1853.

While the cost of moving cargo by canal was far cheaper than any other method, including railroad, canals were far more expensive to build and maintain. The state of Indiana issued bonds to underwrite the Wabash and Erie and nearly went bankrupt paying interest during the long construction period. The railroad was better suited for

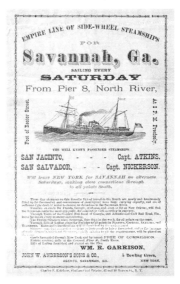

The Empire Line, which offered scheduled passenger service between New York and Savannah, was one of the many steamship lines that reestablished commercial contact between the North and South after the Civil War. This flyer, ca. 1870, makes clear that railroads served to increase maritime trade as they linked inland regions to seaports like Savannah. By 1876, the Empire Line's two iron-hulled steamships, *San Jacinto* and *San Salvador*, would be owned by the Central Railroad of Georgia. (Mystic Seaport, G.W. Blunt White Library, Jennifer M. Stich photo)

1817-50, great age of canal construction, with nearly 4,000 miles in use by the time railroad construction supersedes these "artificial rivers"

1818, steamboat *Walk-in-the-Water* enters service on Lake Erie as the first steamboat on the Great Lakes

1824-29, Chesapeake and Delaware Canal connects Chesapeake Bay and Delaware Bay

1829, first Welland Canal in Canada opened to carry water traffic around Niagara Falls between Lake Ontario and Lake Erie

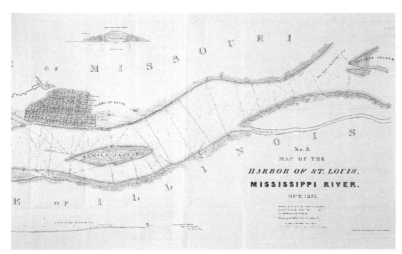

Like ocean harbors, river ports were subject to shoaling and other changes that disrupted traffic. The U.S. Army Corps of Engineers was given responsibility for maintaining navigation early in the 1800s. When the "harbor" of St. Louis got too shallow, Captain Robert E. Lee was assigned to survey the site and propose a solution. He recommended building a dyke downriver from Bloody Island to narrow and speed up the river so it would not drop its silt in the navigation channel. The Army Corps of Engineers grew ever more ambitious, after the Civil War proposing a continuous series of levees along the lower Mississippi to contain the river for navigation. The Mississippi has been trying to break free of its levees ever since. (Mystic Seaport, G.W. Blunt White Library)

23

1836-48, construction of Illinois and Michigan Canal, which first connected Lake Michigan at Chicago with Illinois River connection to the Mississippi, linking Great Lakes to the Mississippi River system

1845, barges first introduced for bulk cargoes on the Ohio River

1848, Pacific Mail Steamship Company inaugurates coastal steamboat service on the West Coast, carrying passengers, freight, and U.S. Mail

1853-55, construction of locks at Sault Ste. Marie, Michigan, allows direct navigation between Lakes Superior and Huron

1859, steamboat service available from St. Louis to Ft. Benton, Montana, 2,000 miles up the Missouri River

1872, establishment of Yellowstone Park, the world's first national park, prominently featuring the Yellowstone River

1873-75, construction of the Eads Bridge at St. Louis, the first bridge across the Mississippi

1878-96, construction of locks around Columbia River Cascades extends navigation up the river

1879, Mississippi River Commission established to manage levees and flood-control efforts on the Mississippi

1881, enlarged lock at Sault Ste. Marie, Michigan, permits large-scale shipment of iron ore from Minnesota to Cleveland, Ohio, for expanding U.S. iron and steel industry

Whether on the ocean, the rivers, or the Great Lakes, steam power revolutionized water transportation in the 1800s. Launched at Detroit in 1847, the side-wheel steamboat *Michigan* carried passengers and freight on the 750-mile run between Buffalo, Detroit, and Green Bay, Wisconsin, providing reliable scheduled service for 17 years. (Mystic Seaport, 95.115)

The 395-foot, steel-hulled schooner *Thomas W. Lawson* was designed as the ultimate in efficient coastal coal carriers. The only seven-masted schooner ever built, she was launched in 1902 and could be sailed by a crew of just 16. For five years the *Lawson* delivered coal from Hampton Roads, Virginia, to Boston. Although she was a profitable carrier, she proved to be difficult to sail in coastal waters. Converted to an oil tanker, she was wrecked during her first voyage across the Atlantic. Within a few years, steam-powered coal ships even larger than this would begin to replace the sailing coal schooners that delivered energy in the form of coal to residents of the Northeast. With the shift from coal to oil since World War II, tankers have replaced colliers on these coastal runs. Nathaniel L. Stebbins photographed the *Lawson* in 1902. (Mystic Seaport, 83.23.1)

As the gateway to navigation between Lake Superior and the other Great Lakes, the first lock around the rapids at Sault Ste. Marie, Michigan, was opened in 1855. During the nation's industrial expansion after the Civil War, iron ore shipped out of the port of Duluth passed through the "Soo Locks" in such quantities that this short stretch of water was among the busiest waterways in the world at the end of the 1800s. In this view from the 1890s, an innovative whaleback bulk carrier passes through the 800-foot-long Poe Lock, one of the increasingly large locks built to accommodate the ore trade. Seaworthy and easy to construct, the strange-looking whalebacks were briefly popular on the Great Lakes before their size limitations made them obsolete for carrying iron ore. (Mystic Seaport, 94.102.2)

passenger and local service. Perfected during the canal era, railroads had exceeded canal mileage by the 1850s. Only the Erie Canal and the coal canals remained profitable after the Civil War.

The Great Lakes also became major transportation arteries. Sailing vessels had plied the Lakes since La Salle launched the *Griffon* in 1679, and traders, collectively known as voyageurs, traveled the Great and smaller northern lakes in their cargo canoes. The steamboat *Walk-in-the-Water* introduced steam power on the Great Lakes in 1818, and thereafter passenger and cargo steamboats connected Buffalo, Detroit, Green Bay, and Chicago. The falls of the St. Mary's River prevented ships from entering Lake Superior. In the 1850s the state of Michigan underwrote construction of a lock at Sault Ste. Marie, opening commerce to the westernmost lake.

As the nation became an increasing producer of raw materials after the Civil War, water transportation was increasingly devoted to bulk shipment. Tremendous quantities of grain from the Great Plains traveled the Great Lakes from Chicago to Buffalo by ship and barge. The opening of the "iron ranges" in northern Michigan

1890-1910, transitional period on the Mississippi River system, with shift from large passenger- and freight-carrying steamboats to towboats pushing strings of barges carrying bulk cargoes

1904-14, construction of the Panama Canal

1914, opening of Cape Cod Canal eliminates hazardous passage around Cape Cod for coastal navigation

Opening of Houston Ship Canal, giving ocean shipping access to petroleum center of Houston, Texas

1915, construction of Celilo Locks on Columbia River permits navigation as far upstream as Lewiston, Idaho

1920-40, Army Corps of Engineers constructs dam and lock systems on upper Mississippi and Ohio Rivers to provide consistent nine-foot water depth for navigation from Pittsburgh to St. Paul

1923, establishment of Inland Waterways Corporation (also known as Federal Barge Lines), which helped revitalize commercial shipping on the Mississippi and Ohio Rivers

1927, a great flood inundates much of lower Mississippi River Valley

1933, Illinois Waterway permits large-scale barge traffic between Chicago and the Mississippi River

1933-63, dam construction on Tennessee River extends navigation to 750 miles

1937, end of Long Island Sound passenger steamboat service

25

Photographed along the river-
bank at Decatur, Alabama, the
153-foot steamboat *R.C. Gunter*
reflects the importance of
river transportation to inland
communities. She is stacked
with cotton bales, and boxes of
merchandise and bags of produce
wait to be moved. Launched at
Chattanooga, Tennessee, in 1886,
the *Gunter* ran on the Tennessee
River before serving on the
Illinois River and out of Kansas
City before being broken up at
age 21. (Mystic Seaport, 92.43.1)

1959, opening of St. Lawrence
Seaway in Canada, which permits
large ocean-going ships to enter
the Great Lakes and to travel the
2,342 miles between the Atlantic
Ocean and Duluth, Minnesota

1975, Lower Granite Dam on
Snake River allows expanded
grain shipments by barge from
Lewiston, Idaho, to Portland,
Oregon

1993, a great flood interrupts
navigation on upper Mississippi

and inland from Duluth, Minnesota, produced millions of
tons of iron ore for shipment 900 miles down the Lakes to
the steel mills near the port of Cleveland. Steamships
exceeded sailing vessels on the Lakes by the 1870s, and
they soon developed a characteristic form, with a long,
narrow iron or steel hull to navigate the locks, the pilothouse at the bow, a deckhouse at the stern, and many
cargo hatches in the deck. Improvements in unloading
equipment, especially the Huelett Unloader—a very large
steam shovel—encouraged the construction of larger
ships, which reached 600 feet long after 1900, and 1,000
feet long 70 years later. Until ice closed the Great Lakes
to navigation each winter, the "Soo Locks" were one of the
world's busiest waterways, and the locks were enlarged
repeatedly to accommodate larger ships.

By the 1880s, Ohio and Mississippi River steamboats
were turning into towboats, pushing barges of cargo
rather than carrying it on board.

In the last decades of the nineteenth century railroad
construction on the northern plains drew commerce
away from the upper reaches of the Missouri River, and in
the twentieth century the Missouri was dammed for
irrigation and flood control, limiting navigation to the 750
miles below Sioux City, South Dakota.

By the 1920s, railroads competed successfully with steamboat passenger service in many areas. From Chesapeake
Bay to Maine, local steamboat lines consolidated and cut
back as railroads and expanding automobile and truck

All along the Mississippi River system, from Pennsylvania to South Dakota and Minnesota to Louisiana, towboats and their strings of barges still crowd the rivers with traffic. Here on the Monongahela River south of Pittsburgh, Pennsylvania, in 1999, the towboat *R.L. Ireland* pushes coal barges to a power plant for the Consolidation Coal Company, passing the 78-foot towboat *John L. Rozance* (below), with empty barges headed upstream. (Fred Calabretta photos)

traffic offered more convenient local transportation. Even most of the premier routes—the Fall River Line that served travelers between New York and Boston, the Hudson River Day Line, the Old Bay Line on Chesapeake Bay, and the lines that linked Los Angeles, San Francisco, Portland, and Seattle—had ceased operating by World War II.

But if passengers took to land, the U.S. Army Corps of Engineers and various regional authorities oversaw the "canalization" of many of the rivers of the Mississippi system. By removing obstructions and building dams and locks to control the water level, they extended reliable water transportation from Pittsburgh and Knoxville in the east to St. Paul and Sioux City in the north, or via the Illinois River to Chicago, to Oklahoma City in the west, and to New Orleans in the south. Carried in strings of barges pushed by towboats, the commodities of America—corn, wheat, oil, coal, and iron—could travel the rivers with fewer delays caused by low or high water. On the West Coast, locks and dams on the Columbia River extended navigation 800 miles inland to Lewiston, Idaho.

Things have changed greatly in recent years, but the nation's waterways remain streams of progress. Although ore shipments on the Great Lakes have declined, the St. Lawrence Seaway has made the Lakes a literal fourth coast, with shipping connections around the world. The fleet of coastal traders has been largely superseded by truck, rail, air, and pipeline shipment of goods, but petroleum, chemicals, and other bulk cargoes still travel efficiently by ship along the coast. And the Mississippi River may still rage in flood stage, but the entire river system has been engineered into a giant canal with levees and locks to control the water and float long strings of barges carrying more cargo than ever before.

COLEMAN'S CALIFORNIA LINE
FOR
SAN FRANCISCO.

THE NEW AND ELEGANT EXTREME CLIPPER SHIP

RANGOON

A. P. BOYD, Commander,

Is now rapidly loading at Pier 15 East River,

FOOT OF WALL ST.

This splendid vessel has been built with the greatest care, EXPRESSLY FOR THE CALIFO

Part Three

CONNECTING AMERICA TO THE WORLD

The high seas were America's first avenues to the world, and they remain our most important links today. Take a look at your shoes, your clothes, your camera. . . Do you know where they came from, and how they got to America?

The idea of a "world economy" is not new. Even though America is blessed with rich natural resources, our nation's well-being has always depended on the ships and sailors who traveled the world's sea-lanes to the world's markets.

Trade across the Atlantic began with the first colonists in their tiny sailing vessels from Europe. Today huge motor ships cross the Pacific in just days, carrying goods that most of us take for granted.

Since mariners first ventured across the Atlantic and Pacific Oceans during the age of exploration in the fifteenth and sixteenth centuries, the great ocean highways have connected Americans to the world. As avenues of commercial and cultural exchange, the sea-lanes were the essential links by which we shaped and distinguished an American culture.

With the shift to passenger travel by air and the development of instantaneous worldwide communication during the past 50 years, we have forgotten that sea trade is still our principal link to the world's markets.

America is a nation of trade. The European exploration that encountered these shores after 1492, and the colonization that settled them after 1607, was based on commerce. The English colonies that predominated on the Atlantic Coast were part of a mercantile economic system, providing raw materials for the mother country, then consuming goods produced in the mother country. Sea trade made the system possible. New England fish and timber, Middle Atlantic grain and furs, and Southern tobacco, indigo, and rice flowed to Europe, and all sorts of manufactured goods, from cloth to glass and iron, came back to be distributed through American seaports. These entrepôts of goods and information—for ships were the swiftest carriers of news and information as well—became the cultural centers of North America and the first true cities on the continent.

Illustration on page 28: The
name of the 1862 ship *Rangoon*
symbolized the lure of Asia
in the American maritime
economy. The demand for tea
contributed to the development
of fast-sailing "clipper" ships,
which earned such a reputation
for quality that even full-bodied
ships like the *Rangoon* might be
advertised as clippers to attract
business. (Mystic Seaport, G.W.
Blunt White Library; Judy
Beisler photo)

In his "Elegy on the Times" (1774), poet John Trumbull emphasized the maritime connections that had created Boston's prosperity.

Oh, Boston! late with ev'ry pleasure crown'd,
Where Commerce triumph'd on the favoring gales,
And each pleas'd eye, that rov'd in prospect round,
Hail'd thy bright spires and bless'd thy op'ning sails!

Thy plenteous marts with rich profusion smil'd;
Thy gay throng crowded in thy spacious streets;
From either Ind thy cheerful stores were fill'd;
Thy ports were gladden'd with unnumber'd fleets.

For there more fair than in their native vales,
Tall groves of masts arose in beauteous pride;
The waves were whiten'd by the swelling sails,
And plenty wafted on the neighb'ring tide. . . .

Revolution, which was largely fostered in those seaports and partly tied to the trade restrictions imposed on the American colonies by England, resulted in the expulsion of the new American states from the trading family of the British Empire. The United States was not a self-sufficient nation, so trade by sea became essential. Adventurous merchants sent out their ships to find new trading partners. In the Caribbean, Europe, Africa, and Asia they sought markets for American materials where they could get the sugar, rum, cloth, slaves, tea, and spices they had come to depend upon.

Beginning in 1784, Americans established trade with China, obtaining tea, porcelain, and silks for wealthy Americans. In exchange, China wanted little that America could supply, so China traders carried out American silver, ginseng, and furs obtained on the Northwest Coast, or scoured the Pacific for exotic items such as sandalwood or beche de mer (sea slugs) to meet demands in China. The China trade would remain a small but important link between east and west throughout the 1800s.

The trade in goods and passengers across the Atlantic quickly returned to its former prominence. So important was sea trade to the new American nation that the customs duties on imports paid 90 percent of the government budget. From 1792 to 1812, during the Napoleonic Wars between England and France, American merchants found a lucrative niche as "neutral traders," taking advantage of international law to carry goods to both warring nations from their colonies after first landing the goods in the U.S. temporarily to make them "American." Even though more than 20 percent of these neutral traders were captured by the warring forces, the trade brought great prosperity to American seaports. But it ended abruptly at the beginning of 1808 when President Thomas Jefferson declared an embargo on U.S. ships to force England and France to recognize U.S. rights and to end the British practice of "impressing" sailors from American ships into the Royal Navy with the claim that they were British subjects. Trade resumed after a year, but the issues were not resolved until the War of 1812.

American trade expanded greatly after the War of 1812. The ships launched in increasing size and number by U.S. shipyards were operated either as regular traders, sailing between the same ports voyage after voyage, or as tramps, sailing wherever a profitable cargo could be carried. A successful captain was a businessman as well as a sailor. Representing his ship's owners, who were too far away to consult, he had to decide on cargoes and routes based on his best guesses about world markets, negotiate freight rates and insurance, manage his crews, and finally navigate his ship safely and quickly to the next port.

To improve North Atlantic trade, a New York firm in 1817 introduced packet service, operating their sailing vessels on schedule, whether full or not. Introduced by the Black Ball Line, the packet concept spread until most major European and American ports were linked by regular packet service.

The 163-foot bark *Martha Davis*, built at East Boston in 1873, was commanded by Captain Timothy Benson in the trade with Asia from 1877 to 1889. Captain Benson's daughter Clara wrote of the vessel: "She had the trim, lovely lines of the old clippers, and always on the high seas and in foreign ports was as exquisitely kept as a yacht. . . . Her after cabin was paneled in bird's eye maple with trimmings of rosewood, and the door frames were pilasters with Corinthian finish at the top touched off with gilding. She looked and felt like an aristocrat of the seas. Like all ships, she had a distinct personality of her own. Walking her deck as it rose rhythmically with the tossing of the sea, I always thought of her as a living, breathing, creature. She became a dear, sympathetic playmate to me, and I used often to bestow little love pats on her rail and hold long secret conversations with her." Despite her good looks, the *Martha Davis* earned her way carrying cargoes like coal, kerosene, iron, hides, sugar, and tea. A Chinese artist painted the *Martha Davis* sailing off Hong Kong. (Mystic Seaport, 85.103.2; Mary Anne Stets photo)

Direct trade between America and China began in 1784 when the ship *Empress of China* left New York for Canton, carrying lead, lumber, cotton cloth, ginseng, and silver specie. A year later she returned to New York with a cargo of tea, silks, and porcelain, including this punch bowl purchased by the ship's carpenter, John Morgan. (Mystic Seaport, 38.77; Mary Anne Stets photo)

Canton (Guangzhou) was the center of China's trade with foreign nations until the 1840s. The Chinese restricted foreign traders to a small section of the city, where they worked and lived in buildings called factories or "hongs." Negotiating through influential Chinese hong merchants, they sold their goods and purchased tea and other Chinese products, which were sent downriver to the waiting merchant ships. As trade expanded, opium took on increasing importance among the few outside goods of economic importance to the Chinese. When Chinese authorities attempted to stop the trade in opium, war erupted between China and Great Britain. As a condition of peace, Britain required the opening of five treaty ports, including Shanghai, and established the British colony of Hong Kong. By the 1850s these other ports, and especially Hong Kong, had replaced Canton as the entrepôts for trade with China. A Chinese artist painted the hongs at Canton, with their national flags flying, ca. 1850. (Mystic Seaport, 54.590)

Scheduled service became somewhat easier with the development of reliable ocean steamships after the American steamer *Savannah* demonstrated the possibility of crossing the Atlantic with sail-assisted steam power in 1819. The British Cunard Line established reliable transatlantic steam service in the 1830s, with large U.S. wooden steamships following in the late 1840s, supported by U.S. Mail subsidies. Edward K. Collins, the leading operator of American sailing packets, set standards for transatlantic steamship service with his grand Collins liners in the 1850s, but the loss of two ships, and the high costs of operation, put the line out of business in 1858.

By the 1850s America's deep-water merchant fleet rivaled Britain's in size and quality of ships. Large, full-bodied packet ships and regular traders crisscrossed the Atlantic while smaller tramps wandered between ports. Sleek, heavily rigged ships nicknamed "clippers" had been developed since the 1840s, first to rush home with tea from China; then, after the gold rush, to combine that service with the delivery of goods to the growing communities of California.

Southern cotton had become the nation's leading commodity, much of it traveling from New Orleans (the country's second-leading port), Mobile, or Charleston to European textile mills aboard hundreds of large American sailing ships. The nation's ships also maintained significant trade with Cuba, South America, and Asia.

American homes reflected the range of sea trade: cotton cloth from England or India, silk from China, ceramics from England or China, copper kettles from Europe, shoes made from South American hides, wine from France, tea from China, coffee from South America, sugar from the Caribbean islands, and fruit from as far away as the Mediterranean. Even the rails for the growing American railroad network came to America by ship. By 1858 nearly 75 percent of U.S. foreign trade was carried in American ships.

Decades of maritime growth were followed by an economic panic in 1857 and then the Civil War. During the war, Confederate commerce raiders stalked Northern ships to destroy the commerce of the Union. As a result, a

Clara Benson (1870-1940) made five voyages with her shipmaster father to Asian ports on board the *Martha Davis* between the ages of seven and seventeen. A Chinese artist painted this portrait. (Mystic Seaport, 85.103.4)

1808, embargo on foreign trade imposed by President Thomas Jefferson to avoid harassment of U.S. ships by British and French

1817, Black Ball Line introduces regularly scheduled transatlantic packet service between New York and Liverpool, England

1819, SS *Savannah* makes first transatlantic crossing by a steamship

1825-55, heyday of transatlantic sailing packets

1845-60, cotton is principal U.S. export

Clipper ship era in the U.S., which reaches the height of extreme designs during the 1849-53 California gold rush

Similar to the officers' quarters of the bark *Martha Davis* as described by Clara Benson, the after cabin of the Down Easter *Benj. F. Packard*, built in 1882, has been restored at Mystic Seaport to represent the vessels that characterized the nation's overseas trading efforts after the Civil War. (Mystic Seaport; B. Smith photo)

When the American merchant marine reached its height before the Civil War, well over 100,000 sailors worked on U.S. ocean traders. This photograph of the watch gathered around the halyard used to raise and lower the main topgallant yard on the bark *Alice*, ca. 1900, suggests the conditions for mariners under sail in the nineteenth century. Working alternating four-hour watches day and night, eating salted provisions, sometimes suffering abuse by tyrannical officers, and often spending months at sea between ports, the sailor's life combined both the adventure of travel and the boredom of routines at sea, the perils of storms at sea and the specialized skills to handle a ship in all conditions. Until the 1850s, seafaring offered opportunities for young men to advance and make their fortunes at sea. As the merchant marine shrank and opportunities declined, the general seafaring population became less skilled and more marginalized. Federal legislation helped reduce the physical and financial abuse of sailors, but the romanticized image of the "jolly tar" no longer fit the reality. (Mystic Seaport, 96.113.1.11)

1850, Collins Line introduces U.S. luxury transatlantic passenger and mail service between New York and Liverpool with wooden side-wheel steamships

1861-65, "flight from the flag" to avoid high insurance rates and possible destruction by Confederate commerce raiders during Civil War results in sale of more than 30 percent of U.S. merchant fleet to foreign owners

1867, Pacific Mail Steamship Company introduces regular U.S. transpacific passenger and freight service from San Francisco to Hong Kong, via Honolulu and Yokohama

1869, opening of Suez Canal favors European steamship trade with Asia

1870-90, era of "Down Easters," large wooden sailing ships mostly built in Maine, which carry bulk cargoes between the East and West Coasts, take American goods to Asia, and deliver California grain to Europe

large proportion of the U.S. fleet was sold to foreign owners, never to return to the American flag.

After this, American entrepreneurs found it more profitable to develop raw materials like coal and iron, or to produce steel or textiles, or build railroads, than to operate merchant ships. Trade through American ports continued to expand, but more and more of it was carried in foreign-flag ships, especially British iron and steel sailing and steam ships, which were cheaper to insure and operate than American wooden ones. The Pacific Mail Steamship Company did establish regular passenger and freight service between San Francisco, Japan, and China in 1867, but most of the American ocean shipping in operation after the Civil War was partially involved in coastal trade, which was protected from foreign competition.

34

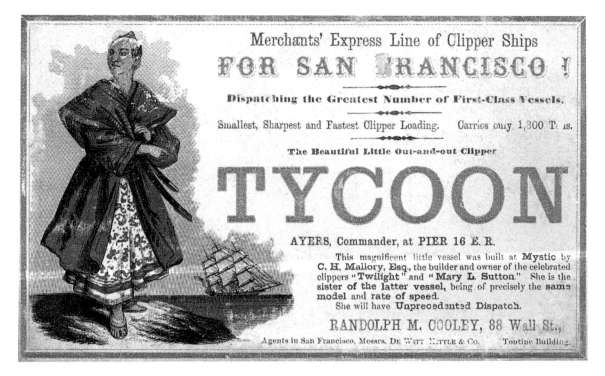

Merchants' Express Line of Clipper Ships
FOR SAN FRANCISCO !

Dispatching the Greatest Number of First-Class Vessels.

Smallest, Sharpest and Fastest Clipper Loading.   Carries only 1,300 Tons.

The Beautiful Little Out-and-out Clipper

TYCOON

AYERS, Commander, at PIER 16 E. R.

This magnificent little vessel was built at Mystic by C. H. Mallory, Esq., the builder and owner of the celebrated clippers "Twilight" and "Mary L. Sutton." She is the sister of the latter vessel, being of precisely the same model and rate of speed.
She will have Unprecedented Dispatch.

RANDOLPH M. COOLEY, 88 Wall St.,

Agents in San Francisco, Messrs. DE WITT KITTLE & Co.   Tontine Building.

Named for the Japanese word for ruler or shogun, the bark *Tycoon* was built at Mystic, Connecticut, in 1860 for the cotton trade. When the Civil War interrupted that profitable trade she began carrying cargo between New York and San Francisco. In April 1864 the *Tycoon* was captured and burned by the *Alabama*, becoming the last of 64 U.S. merchant ships destroyed by that Confederate commerce raider during the Civil War. (Mystic Seaport, G.W. Blunt White Library)

For example, the large square-rigged "Down Easters" (largely built down east in Maine), which represented the American merchant marine from the 1860s through the 1880s, often made one leg of their voyages carrying cargo from New York to San Francisco, which foreign ships could not do, before continuing on to Asia, or carrying California wheat or Peruvian guano (concentrated bird dung used for fertilizer) to Europe or the East Coast.

Although American financiers owned large shares of the European transatlantic steamship lines, including the Cunard and White Star lines through J.P. Morgan's International Mercantile Marine Corporation, the U.S. did not attempt to build a large, modern fleet of ocean steamships until the European fleets were decimated by U-boat warfare during World War I. A nationalized shipbuilding effort to construct standardized ships, overseen by the U.S. Shipping Board, brought the U.S. to the top of the maritime world by 1921. To sustain an active merchant marine the Jones Act of 1920 called for the Shipping Board to oversee the operation of U.S. ships and for the nation to subsidize its merchant marine.

1875-92, first efforts to establish sailors' unions result in National Seaman's Union

1888, Standard Oil Company builds first U.S. oil tanker, *Standard*

1892, British-built *City of Paris* and *City of New York* given U.S. registry, making them first modern U.S. ocean liners, followed by U.S.-built *St. Louis* and *St. Paul*

1894, steam-powered tonnage exceeds sail-powered tonnage in U.S. merchant marine for first time

1899, New York is leading U.S. port

1902, J.P. Morgan establishes International Mercantile Marine Corporation, which soon controls a million tons of shipping through managing ownership of 20 percent of the European and American transatlantic steamship lines, including the White Star, Red Star, Leyland, and American Lines and a major portion of the Holland-America Line, before going bankrupt in 1914

1904-14, construction of the Panama Canal, which changes Atlantic-Pacific trading patterns

1910, reflecting continuing decline, U.S.-registered deep-water fleet makes up only 2 percent of world shipping

With the shift from sail to steam, seafaring became specialized into deck work, engine-room work, and the steward's work of food preparation and housekeeping. Aboard the freighter *Flying Clipper*, one of the ship's three messmen serves sailors of the deck department their noon meal in this 1948 photograph. Cargo ships like the *Flying Clipper*, designed in the 1930s by the U.S. Maritime Commission, were the first American ships to provide roomy quarters for sailors in the ship's superstructure rather than in a cramped forecastle. The station bill on the bulkhead lists the emergency stations and lifeboat assignments for up to 46 members of the deck department, engineering department, and steward's department. For deck work, the *Flying Clipper* was rated to carry a bosun, eight skilled able-bodied seamen, and a couple of less-skilled ordinary seamen (Negative 121871F, © Mystic Seaport Museum, Inc., Rosenfeld Collection)

Although they were larger and powered by engines, cargo ships of 1950 resembled sailing ships of 1850 in the way cargo of all shapes and sizes was stowed in their holds. This view into the number 2 hatch of the 465-foot Farrell Lines freighter *African Endeavor* suggests the mixture, and the need for large gangs of longshoremen to maneuver cargo in and out. The ship's masts and cargo booms, and electric winches around each hatch, permit loading and unloading under a variety of conditions, but the process is slow and labor intensive. Within 20 years such ships would be obsolete, as the revolutionary shift to containerized cargo after 1956 changed ship design, port design, and the requirements of shipboard and alongshore labor. (Negative 124797F, © Mystic Seaport Museum, Inc., Rosenfeld Collection)

36

Among the ships of the enlarged U.S. fleet were an increasing number of oil tankers. Petroleum in the form of kerosene had been a major commodity of trade to Asia since the 1870s. Later, the internal combustion engine required increasing quantities of gasoline, and steamships themselves began to burn oil rather than coal in their boilers. As the worldwide demand for petroleum increased, and oilfields were developed around the world, sea transport of oil became essential. In later years, after the Second World War, American oil companies often registered their tankers under "flags of convenience" in nations such as Panama or Liberia to reduce the costs of operation.

Laws to improve conditions for American sailors after the Civil War culminated in the La Follette Seamen's Act of 1915. Even during the age of sailing ships, food and living conditions were somewhat better aboard American ships. But increasing efforts to improve the lot of sailors, and to unionize them to protect their rights, made their ships less competitive on the high seas, where cost of operation is a major factor in obtaining charters to carry goods.

Even with subsidies, the oversupply of ships from the First World War and competition with foreign fleets forced the American fleet into decline by the time of the Great Depression after 1929. As one of President Franklin Roosevelt's efforts to rebuild the U.S. economy, Congress passed the Merchant Marine Act of 1936, which established the U.S. Maritime Commission to oversee construction of a modern fleet. The Commission developed standard ship types, and construction had begun when the U.S. entered World War II.

Wartime demands for shipping to carry troops, munitions, supplies, and fuel were increased by the heavy loss of U.S. ships to German U-boats early in the war. Around the country, the Maritime Commission established new shipyards. In the greatest shipbuilding effort in history, U.S. shipyards launched more than 5,700 ships between 1939 and 1945. More than 2,700 of them were the famous Liberty ships, built quickly and cheaply for wartime needs. Like the ships themselves, American merchant mariners were freely sacrificed during the world war. With 6,000 sailors lost at sea, the casualty rate for merchant seamen was actually higher than it was for U.S. Navy sailors.

The U.S. ended World War II with the world's largest merchant fleet. Within a few years, however, Asian and

1915, La Follette Seamen's Act protects rights of U.S. sailors and establishes safety requirements for U.S. oceangoing ships

1917-21, U.S. Shipping Board oversees nationwide World War I shipbuilding boom

1920, Merchant Marine Act (Jones Act) authorizes sale of government-built ships to promote expansion of U.S. merchant marine

1936, Merchant Marine Act establishes subsidy system to make U.S. shipping costs competitive and provides labor standards for seamen

1938-45, U.S. Maritime Commission oversees construction of world's largest merchant fleet to meet wartime demands for cargo vessels, including more than 2,700 Liberty ships

1952, SS *United States*, last great U.S. transatlantic liner, enters service and captures blue riband symbolizing fastest ship on the Atlantic

1956, Malcolm McLean begins carrying trailer-truck bodies on shipboard, introducing concept of containerization

1957, for the first time, more people cross the Atlantic by airplane than by ship

1959, launch of first and only U.S. nuclear-powered merchant ship, SS *Savannah*

1969, SS *United States* retired, ending regular U.S. transatlantic liner service

1970, Merchant Marine Act encourages construction and operation of new and efficient U.S. merchant fleet

1973, American President Lines terminates transpacific passenger service

1990, Oil Pollution Act, in response to 1989 *Exxon Valdez* stranding, requires double-hull construction for U.S. oil tankers, first of which are launched from U.S. shipyards in 1996

1999, New Orleans, Louisiana, is leading U.S. port by volume of cargo; Los Angeles is leading U.S. port by value of cargo

European nations had rebuilt their fleets, subsidized their operation, and could operate their ships more cheaply.

Although the U.S. merchant marine began to decline again in the 1950s, an American innovation has revolutionized the world's merchant shipping since that time. For thousands of years, cargo had arrived at the wharf in a great variety of containers, which required much time to load into and unload from the holds of traditional break-bulk ships. Bringing a concept from land transportation, trucker Malcolm McLean proposed carrying cargo in standard-size containers that could be stacked efficiently on shipboard. He experimented with reinforced trailer-truck bodies in 1956, and within a few years his Sea-Land company had proven that "intermodal" transportation worked. A container could be packed, for example, at a factory near Hong Kong, put on a ship for delivery to Los Angeles, unloaded onto a truck or railroad car, and carried to Chicago to pass through customs before being opened for distribution of the contents to local stores. By the 1960s, the old break-bulk ships that carried boxes, barrels, and bales were obsolete.

This revolution in shipping had great impact ashore, where the traditional downtown seaport of wharves and warehouses quickly became obsolete. Prosperous seaports are now vast parking lots, away from downtown, with huge cranes to hoist containers, and with truck and railroad access to move them on shore. The gangs of longshoremen who maneuvered cargo in and out of ships' holds have been replaced by small teams, with most of the work done by a crane operator, directed by a computer operator. The efficiency of this operation can support containerships that are more than twice the size of the old break-bulk ships.

Other specialized ships, such as car carriers, self-unloaders, liquid chemical carriers, and supertankers have further altered trade patterns and seaport design. For example, the largest oil tankers "land" at the Louisiana Offshore Oil Port, a pumping station located 18 miles off the Louisiana coast. As the ships swing at their moorings, oil is pumped into a undersea pipeline that carries it to storage reservoirs in underground salt domes. Many Asian automobiles arrive in the U.S. aboard boxy "ro-ro" (roll-on, roll-off) ships that are like floating parking garages.

Innovation aside, the U.S. fleet has not flourished since the early 1950s. Since then, the federal government has at

The 903-foot containership *President Kennedy* unloads cargo from Asia at the containerport in Seattle, Washington. Containers are made in standard sizes 8 feet square and 20, 40, 45, or 48 feet long. A ship's container capacity is measured in TEUs—20-foot equivalent units—and a C10 ship like the *President Kennedy* can carry 4,300 TEUs stacked eight high in the hold and up to five high on deck. The ship's 57,000 horsepower engine drives it across the ocean at 24 knots, and the large gantry cranes in a containerport unload and load the ship in a matter of hours. The wide beam of 129 feet makes C10s very stable, but also exceeds the width of the Panama Canal locks. Much of the nation's Pacific trade is carried by APL (American President Lines), which derived from the Pacific Mail Steamship Company, founded in 1848. Since APL, with its fleet of modern containerships, was purchased by Neptune Orient Lines, Ltd., in 1997 and Sea-Land was purchased in l999, the Matson Line operates the only large containership fleet flying the American flag. (Clevenger Photo 970516.3, Courtesy APL)

times favored ship operators with subsidies to help them compete with subsidized foreign ships and has proposed that the merchant marine is an essential element of national defense. However between strict regulation and world economic changes beyond the shippers' control, the nation's merchant marine has continued to decline. Shifts in the U.S. economy, with declining production of such commodities as steel and textiles, means that more essential and consumer goods are imported; yet less than 5 percent of the goods we purchase arrive in ships flying the U.S. flag.

There is no question that ocean trade is more important than ever to Americans. Perhaps in a true world economy the U.S. can choose to be a nation of consumers rather than transporters. However, is it wise for a nation built on international trade to give up the means to control that trade?

Part Four
SERVING AT SEA

Millions of Americans have experienced the sea while serving their country in the U.S. Navy. In wartime the navy has defended our coasts and protected America's interests at sea. In peace-time, navy personnel have served as scientists, explorers, diplomats, and humanitarians.

Since the first sea battles of the Revolutionary War, naval history and traditions have enriched virtually all aspects of American life, and the image of a U.S. Navy sailor in uniform has been one of America's most familiar patriotic symbols.

Although the sailor's experience has changed greatly over the years, the men and women of today's U.S. Navy, supported by their families ashore, continue to uphold traditions of the past as they serve their country on the frontiers of the sea.

On the ocean frontier, beyond national boundaries, a nation's interests are represented and defended by its navy. In the face of the British Royal Navy, the world's most powerful sea service, the rebellious North American colonies created the Continental Navy in 1775 to help gain independence at sea. Although that patchwork navy was gradually overwhelmed, the success of such officers as John Paul Jones, and the naval defense of Lake Champlain by Benedict Arnold, contributed much to the new nation's victory in the Revolution. The heroic actions of these naval revolutionaries would later become mythic symbols of American maritime prowess.

The U.S. Constitution called for creation of a national navy, and in 1797 that force was established to protect American interests overseas, fighting the Quasi-War with France, 1798-1800, and the war with Tripoli, 1801-05, to protect American trade at sea. To defend American interests in North America, and to protect the rights of American ships at sea in the face of British naval impressment of American seamen and capture of American ships carrying neutral goods during the Napoleonic Wars, the U.S. declared war on Great Britain in 1812.

41

**America's Guardians at Sea:
A Chronology**

1775, 13 October, Continental
Congress authorizes a
Continental Navy

1776, 3 March, U.S. Marines
capture Nassau, Bermuda, in first
U.S. amphibious operation

Illustration on page 40: Admiral
David Glasgow Farragut (1801-
70) personified the U.S. Navy in
the heroic age of the nineteenth
century. Born in Tennessee,
Farragut became the ward of
Captain David Porter and was
appointed a naval midshipman at
age 10, serving under Porter during the War of 1812 aboard the
USS *Essex*, the first U.S. Navy
vessel to enter the Pacific Ocean.
He served on many of the navy's
duty stations and in 1858 established the Mare Island Navy
Yard near San Francisco in the
new state of California. He was
living in Virginia and close to
retirement when the Civil War
began. Farragut moved north and
was selected to play a prominent
role in President Abraham
Lincoln's "Anaconda Plan" to
defeat the Confederacy by controlling the waterways. Aboard
his flagship, the USS *Hartford*,
Farragut commanded the fleet
that captured New Orleans in
1862 and helped open the
Mississippi River in 1863. In
August 1864 his flotilla won the
Battle of Mobile Bay, sealing that
major Confederate port. In honor
of his wartime successes,
Farragut was named the navy's
first rear admiral in 1862 and first
full admiral in 1866. A year
before Farragut's death, a large
and elegant medium clipper ship
was christened *Great Admiral* in
his honor. This lifelike figurehead
was carefully maintained on the
ship for 37 years, and it was sal-
vaged when the ship was
wrecked on the Oregon coast in
1906. (Mystic Seaport, 58.1095;
Bill Grant photo)

Though far outnumbered, the USS *Constitution* and other
U.S. frigates won prominent victories at sea, and U.S.
Navy flotillas commanded by Oliver Hazard Perry on
Lake Erie and Thomas Macdonough on Lake Champlain
defeated British squadrons to protect the country's
northern border. These naval contributions gave the U.S.
the strength to negotiate a favorable conclusion to the war
and a more secure position in the world order. Ever since,
"Old Ironsides" and the war's naval heroes have been
celebrated as patriotic symbols of the nation.

> *Huzza! for the brave Yankee boys,*
> *Who touch'd up John Bull on lake Erie,*
> *Who gave 'em a taste of our toys,*
> *From the fleet of brave Commodore Perry. . . .*

Brilliant Naval Victory (ballad ca. 1813)

The U.S. Navy's early victories inspired American whalemen to incorporate
patriotic themes in their characteristic art of scrimshaw. An unidentified
scrimshander engraved these sperm whale teeth with views of Commandant
Thomas Macdonough's 1814 victory on Lake Champlain *(top)* and Captain
Oliver H. Perry's 1813 victory on Lake Erie *(bottom)*. Patriotic lithographs by
Nathaniel Currier provided the model for at least the Lake Champlain
engraving. (Mystic Seaport, 41.411, 41.412; Mary Anne Stets and Claire
White Peterson photo)

The U.S. Navy has frequently served a diplomatic role on the frontiers of the sea. In the first half of the nineteenth century, as the U.S. and European powers vied for commercial influence in Asia, Japan remained a closed society, with very limited contact with non-Asian peoples. After California became a state in 1850, merchants and naval planners envisioned regular transpacific steamship travel between California and China. In order to establish a strategic coaling station for American steamships and expand Asian trade, Matthew Calbraith Perry proposed a naval expedition to intimidate Japan into opening its ports. Perry was named commodore of the navy's East Asia Squadron, and in July 1853 steamed into Edo Bay. Since the Japanese had never seen a steamship, Perry made certain that the squadron included three of the navy's new steam frigates. After delivering a letter from President Millard Fillmore proposing friendly relations between the nations, Perry promised to return in the spring for a decision. On 8 March 1854, as shown here in a lithograph by expedition artist Peter B.W. Heine, he landed at Yokohama to negotiate with the Japanese commissioners. Perry's show of force and patient diplomacy resulted in the Treaty of Kanagawa, which pledged peace between the U.S. and Japan, opened two Japanese ports to U.S. vessels needing supplies, and pledged Japanese care for shipwrecked American sailors. On the basis of this peaceful naval initiative, the U.S. and Japan signed a commercial treaty four years later. (Mystic Seaport, 63.350; Mary Anne Stets photo)

For almost 50 years after the War of 1812, the U.S. maintained a small navy that lagged behind European fleets in technological development. In a period of international peace, the navy showed the flag around the world, sporadically patrolled the African coast in pursuit of slave traders, and participated in the short Mexican-American War. Most notably, the navy conducted the 1838-42 U.S. Exploring Expedition, commanded by Lieutenant Charles Wilkes, to collect data and develop commercial relations

1776, 11-13 October, American fleet on Lake Champlain defeated, but delays British invasion of northern New York

1779, August, large American navy fleet lost in Maine's Penobscot Bay

September, "I have not yet begun to fight," Captain John Paul Jones reportedly proclaims as his damaged American ship *Bonhomme Richard* defeats HMS *Serapis* off Flamborough Head, England, in best-known naval engagement of the American Revolution

1785, Continental Navy dissolved; U.S. has no fleet for 12 years

1794, Congress authorizes construction of six frigates

1797, launch of first three frigates, including USS *Constitution*

1798, 30 April, U.S. Congress establishes Department of the Navy

1798-1800, U.S. Navy fights Quasi-War with France

around the Pacific. A decade later, Commodore Matthew C. Perry led a naval squadron to establish relations with Japan.

Despite progressive experiments, the navy was slow to adopt steam power and the screw propeller for its ships. However, Lieutenant Matthew F. Maury's pioneering efforts to chart the oceans' current and weather patterns for the benefit of mariners, and the establishment of the U.S. Naval Academy at Annapolis in 1845, represented the beginnings of a sophisticated, professional navy for the U.S.

While the Civil War was largely a land conflict, naval and maritime efforts had far-reaching effects. The Confederate States of America had little in the way of a merchant marine or sophisticated industry, but the U.S. Navy officers who left the service to go with their home states were particularly bold and innovative. The Confederacy pioneered in the use

George Washington.

ALL patriotic and gallant Seamen, who are desirous to serve and defend their country, are invited to repair to the rendezvous now opened at Providence, and enlist for one year to serve on board the good frigate GEORGE WASHINGTON. The pay is seventeen dollars per month for all able bodied Seamen, with good and abundant rations. A few able bodied landsmen are also wanted. The ship will be at sea in a few weeks, and from the zeal and alacrity of American Seamen, her brave crew wi l no doubt in a few days be completed. *N. B.* Two dollars towards defraying their expences to Providence will be allowed.
Providence, May. 21.

Boston Columbian Centinel, 21 May 1800 (Mystic Seaport, G.W. Blunt White Library)

1801-05, U.S. Navy fights war with Tripoli and other Barbary States of North Africa

1807, 22 June, HMS *Leopard* fires into USS *Chesapeake* over right of impressment, a precipitating factor of the War of 1812

1812, 19 August, USS *Constitution* defeats HMS *Guerrière* in the first U.S. victory of the War of 1812

18 October, USS *Wasp* defeats HMS *Frolic*

25 October, USS *United States* defeats HMS *Macedonian*

29 December, USS *Constitution* defeats HMS *Java*

1813, February, USS *Essex* rounds Cape Horn, the first U.S. Navy vessel to enter the Pacific Ocean

1 June, HMS *Shannon* defeats USS *Chesapeake*, despite mortally wounded Captain James Lawrence's plea, "Don't give up the ship!"

10 September, "We have met the enemy; they are ours," Master Commandant Oliver Hazard Perry reports after his U.S. flotilla on Lake Erie defeats British squadron, ensuring U.S. hold on the northwest

In the overcrowded world of a navy ship, organization and discipline are essential. The crew's comings and goings for their four-hour watch periods and duty assignments were controlled by a noncommissioned petty officer called the boatswain (bosun), who was assisted by several boatswain's mates. This boatswain's mate of the USS *Concord*, on duty in the Mediterranean, 1830-32, displays the distinctive whistle he used to signal the crew. Like many nineteenth-century navy sailors, he has personalized his uniform with decorative embroidery. U.S. Marine E.C. Young painted this watercolor. (Mystic Seaport, G.W. Blunt White Library; Jennifer Stich photo)

Attack of (pseudo) Rebel torpedo boat upon U.S.S. Richmond 22nd Mch.

Naval warfare changed greatly during the Civil War. In March 1864, engineering officer Robert W. Weir sketched the crew of the USS *Richmond* preparing to battle a log, which in the dark appeared to be a Confederate torpedo boat attempting to sink their vessel. The Confederacy used such unconventional tactics as ironclad vessels, torpedoes, and submarines to counter the large, well-armed U.S. fleet, including the *Richmond*, that blockaded the coast to strangle the Southern economy. Wooden sail-and-steam-powered vessels like the *Richmond*, with their rows of cannon, would remain in service for decades after the Civil War, but steam-powered armored vessels, torpedoes, and submarines represented the future of the U.S. Navy. The son of West Point artist Robert W. Weir, and the brother of artists J. Alden and John F. Weir, Robert Weir took his own artistic talents to sea, making several whaling voyages before his naval service during the Civil War. (Mystic Seaport, G.W. Blunt White Library, VFM 1298)

of armored warships, the most notable being the *Virginia*, built on the hulk of the USS *Merrimack*; perfected a floating "torpedo" (exploding mine); constructed the first submarine to sink a warship, the *H.L. Hunley*; and operated a number of highly successful commerce raiders on the high seas, the most destructive being the CSS *Alabama*.

At the same time, the U.S. Navy contributed largely to the preservation of the Union, increasing in size to 51,500 men and more than 600 ships, mostly powered by steam, and establishing a naval blockade of the Southern coast to prevent Confederate trade with Europe. The navy was also instrumental in winning control of the Mississippi River to cut the Confederacy in half, and in capturing or

1814, February, USS *Essex* defeated by British frigates at Valparaiso, Chile

11 September, Thomas Macdonough's fleet on Lake Champlain defeats British fleet, stalling British invasion, and spurs British negotiators to give up territorial claims in America and settle War of 1812

1820-23, U.S. Navy makes first patrols against slave ships on West African coast

1823, U.S. Navy eradicates piracy in the Caribbean

1838-42, Lieutenant Charles Wilkes commands U.S. Exploring Expedition in around-the-world voyage to gather scientific data and seek commercial opportunities in the Pacific

1840-62, U.S. Navy African Squadron operates along west coast of Africa to prevent slave trading by American-flag vessels

45

1841, U.S. Navy launches its first practical steamships, USS *Mississippi* and *Missouri*

1843, U.S. Navy launches its first iron ship, the USS *Michigan,* for service on Great Lakes, and the USS *Princeton,* the first naval vessel designed for screw propulsion

1845, U.S. Congress authorizes establishment of U.S. Naval Academy at Annapolis, Maryland

1850, U.S. Congress abolishes flogging as punishment aboard U.S. Navy ships

1854, 31 March, with Treaty of Kanagawa, Commodore Matthew C. Perry completes negotiations opening Japan to relations with the U.S.

1861, 19 April, with outbreak of Civil War, President Lincoln proclaims blockade of Southern coast, requiring expansion of U.S. Navy from 90 to more than 600 vessels during the war

1862, February, U.S. gunboat flotilla begins to advance on Mississippi, Tennessee, and Cumberland Rivers

6 March, first battle between ironclad warships as USS *Monitor* confronts CSS *Virginia,* which had destroyed three wooden U.S. Navy ships in Hampton Roads, Virginia

April, Union fleet under Admiral David Farragut runs Confederate defenses of Mississippi River Delta, leading to the fall of New Orleans

1 September, U.S. Congress abolishes daily grog (alcohol) ration in the U.S. Navy

As employees, representatives, and seaborne defenders of the American people, naval officers are commissioned by the president in our behalf, "reposing special Trust and Confidence in [their] Patriotism, Valor, Fidelity and Abilities." In peacetime their attention to duty goes largely unnoticed by the population; in war they sometimes earn public acclaim and lasting fame. Alexander C. Rhind (1821-97) entered the navy in 1838. He completed his training as a midshipman in 1845, a few months before the establishment of the U.S. Naval Academy at Annapolis, Maryland. During the Mexican-American War and through the 1850s he rose slowly through the navy with a promotion to lieutenant in 1854. With the outbreak of the Civil War, he began to demonstrate the ideals of a navy officer. Commanding a gunboat on the South Carolina coast, Lieutenant Rhind quickly earned a reputation for bravery and resourcefulness. Commissioned a lieutenant commander by President Abraham Lincoln in February 1863, he took over the new ironclad *Keokuk* in the flotilla attempting to capture Charleston, South Carolina. Boldly attacking Fort Sumter in April 1863, the *Keokuk* was badly damaged by the fort's guns and sank the following day. After duty on Virginia's James River, Rhind received a special assignment in December 1864 to command a vessel loaded with gunpowder that was to be anchored and detonated close to Confederate Fort Fisher, which guarded the approach to Wilmington, North Carolina. With a volunteer crew, Rhind performed this nearly suicidal mission, but could not get the vessel close enough to damage the fort. After his heroic wartime service, Rhind remained in the navy, being promoted to captain in 1870, commodore in 1876, and rear admiral in 1883. When he retired, he had spent more than 45 years in his country's service. In 1938 the navy honored this brave officer when it launched the destroyer *Rhind*. (Mystic Seaport, G.W. Blunt White Library, HFM 111; Jennifer Stich photo)

46

closing the principal Confederate ports. The U.S. Navy also enlisted many African Americans during the war, either free blacks from the North or recently freed slaves from the South, until as many as one out of five sailors were black men fighting for their freedom.

In answer to the Southern ironclads the North also built armored ships, the most innovative being the *Monitor*, which introduced the concept of a rotating gun turret. The result of all of these wartime developments was to make the sailor more and more a part of a machine rather than a heroic individual with traditional seafaring skills.

Herman Melville pondered the effects of naval technology in his poem, "A Utilitarian View of the *Monitor*'s Fight."

Plain be the phrase, yet apt the verse,
More ponderous than nimble;
For since grimed War here laid aside
His Orient pomp, 'twould ill befit
Overmuch to ply
The rhyme's barbaric cymbal.

Hail to victory without the gaud
of glory; zeal that needs no fans
Of banners; plain mechanic power
Plied cogently in War now placed—
Where War belongs—
Among the trades and artisans.

Yet this was battle, and intense—
Beyond the strife of fleets heroic;
Deadlier, closer, calm 'mid storm;
No passion; all went by crank,
Pivot, and screw,
And calculations of caloric.

Needless to dwell; the story's known.
The ringing of those plates on plates
Still ringeth round the world—
The clangor of that blacksmith's fray.
The anvil-din
Resounds this message from the Fates:

War shall yet be, and to the end;
But war-paint shows the streaks of weather;
War yet shall be, but warriors
Are now but operatives; War's made
Less grand than Peace,
And a singe runs through lace and feather.

1863, 4 July, after a year of Union naval attacks and three-month siege, Confederate stronghold of Vicksburg, Mississippi, falls; with surrender of Port Hudson, Louisiana, five days later, the Mississippi River comes under Union control

1864, 17 February, in the first successful submarine attack, CSS *H.L. Hunley* sinks USS *Housatonic* off Charleston, South Carolina, but is lost in the attack

19 June, USS *Kearsarge* sinks CSS *Alabama* off Cherbourg, France, after *Alabama* had destroyed 64 U.S. merchant ships during nearly two years of commerce raiding

5 August, Union fleet under Admiral Farragut aboard USS *Hartford* storms Mobile Bay, with Farragut reportedly ordering, "Damn the torpedoes, full speed ahead," capturing ironclad CSS *Tennessee* and sealing last large Confederate Gulf Coast port

1865, 13-15 January, amphibious assault with naval support captures Fort Fisher, North Carolina, closing last Confederate port on the Atlantic to blockade runners

April, at end of the Civil War U.S. Navy totals more than 600 vessels and 51,500 men

June, CSS *Shenandoah* sinks 24 American whaleships off Alaska before learning of the war's end

1868, USS *Wampanoag* sets ocean speed record with run of almost 18 knots; however, U.S. Navy returns to small-scale force with ironclad monitors for coastal defense and a few wooden sail-and-steam-powered vessels for distant stations

1882, Admiral Robert W. Schufeldt, in command of U.S. Navy squadron, negotiates commercial relations with Korea

The U.S. Navy's traditions of duty, courage, and personal sacrifice at sea are personified by the five Sullivan brothers of Waterloo, Iowa. These sons of first-generation Irish immigrants vowed to join the navy and serve together on the same ship to avenge the death of a friend killed during the attack on Pearl Harbor. "If the worst comes to worst, why we'll have all gone down together," commented the eldest brother, George, already a navy veteran. The Sullivans were assigned to the light cruiser USS *Juneau*. During action in the Solomon Islands, the *Juneau* was torpedoed and sank on 13 November 1942. More than 600 crewmen were lost, including all five of the Sullivans. The brothers' loss is considered the single greatest sacrifice by one family in U.S. military history. This photograph of the Sullivans—(*left to right*) Joseph, 23, Francis, 26, Albert, 19, Madison, 22, and George, 27—aboard the USS *Juneau* was made into a very effective recruiting poster for the U.S. Navy, and their sacrifice has been honored in film and in the naming of U.S. Navy destroyers in 1943 and 1995. (Mystic Seaport, 97.61.1)

Despite the wartime innovation, the reunified United States dismantled much of its naval power after the war and did not become a competitive world naval force until after the navy built its first steel warships in the 1880s and Alfred Thayer Mahan's theory of the strategic significance of sea power became an element of U.S. policy. The modern U.S. Pacific and Atlantic squadrons easily defeated the Spanish navy in the Philippines and Cuba during the Spanish-American War of 1898, and in 1907-09 President Theodore Roosevelt sent the Great White Fleet of U.S. battleships around the world to signal U.S. naval prominence.

At the same time, the U.S. Navy was developing a practical submarine force. Shortly after its supporting role in World War I, the U.S. Navy commissioned the first aircraft carrier as it became clear that the airplane was making the battleship obsolete as the dominant naval vessel. By the time international restrictions on naval strength after World War I were broken during the arms race of the 1930s, the U.S. fleet reflected the need to dominate the air as well as the surface and undersea regions to conduct a naval war.

The U.S. joined the Second World War after the Japanese attack on the Pacific Fleet at Pearl Harbor, Hawai'i, supporting European efforts in the Atlantic while confronting Japanese invasions in the Pacific. The attack at Pearl Harbor emphasized the vulnerability of battleships to air and undersea attack. Although naval guns supported a succession of hard-fought U.S. Marine amphibious assaults on the islands of the South Pacific,

The U.S. Navy enlisted female nurses as early as 1908, and female "yeoman" clerks during World War I. To accommodate the demand for manpower at sea during World War II, the navy established the Women Accepted for Volunteer Emergency Service (WAVES) in 1942. Carol Hurlbutt Norman of Gales Ferry, Connecticut, a secretary, enlisted in the WAVES in February 1943. After her training at the Iowa State Teacher's College, she was assigned to the U.S. Naval Construction Training Center at Davisville, Rhode Island. As in other branches of the navy, her skilled office service as a yeoman freed men for service at sea or in support roles such as the Construction Battalion (Seabees). Her stylish seersucker summer WAVES uniform was designed for the navy with the assistance of fashion consultants. Designed by the Walt Disney Corporation, the fighting bee became the symbol of the Seabees in October 1944. (Mystic Seaport, 97.157; Judy Beisler photo)

1917-18, U.S. Navy plays small role in World War I, supplying submarine chasers for coastal patrol, destroyers for convoy protection against German U-boats, a few battleships to support the British Royal Navy, and minelayers to plant antisubmarine mines

1917, 4 May, Commander Joseph Taussig leads first U.S. Navy destroyer force to Great Britain, reporting, "We are ready now, sir....This is war, and we are ready to go to sea immediately"

1917-19, women accepted into U.S. Naval Reserve as clerks to free men for sea service

1921, in aerial bombing demonstrations, General William B. Mitchell demonstrates vulnerability of battleships to aircraft attack

1922, Washington Treaties limit armaments of world powers, resulting in reductions in naval forces

USS *Langley* commissioned as first U.S. Navy aircraft carrier

1938, 17 May, Vinson Act authorizes billion-dollar expansion of U.S. Navy several years after Germany and Japan withdrew from arms limitation treaties

1941, September, though still neutral, U.S. Navy destroyers accompanying North Atlantic convoys come under German U-boat attack and are ordered to "shoot on sight"

7 December, Japanese surprise air attack on U.S. Pacific Fleet at Pearl Harbor, Hawai'i, damages or sinks eight battleships. U.S. declares war on Japan the next day, and enters war against Germany three days later

1942, WAVES (Women Accepted for Volunteer Emergency Service) established to enlist women for clerical duties in U.S. Navy

February, Japanese forces defeat U.S. Navy in Battle of the Java Sea

May, U.S. Navy stalls Japanese advance in the South Pacific at the Battle of the Coral Sea, a battle between aircraft carrier task forces that is the first naval engagement in which the opposing fleets never see one another

3-6 June, U.S. Navy turns back Japanese advance through central Pacific in Battle of Midway

August-February 1943, land and sea battles result in U.S. victory at Guadalcanal in Solomon Islands

1943, 7 February, wounded and left on the conning tower of the submarine *Growler* during a surface attack, Commander Howard W. Gilmore gives up his life to save his ship, ordering, "Take her down!"

March-August, U.S. Navy stalls Japanese advance into Aleutian Islands of Alaska

June-December, U.S. Navy and Marines secure the Solomon Islands

July-August, U.S. Navy supports invasion of Sicily

November-November 1944, U.S. Navy and Marines assault Japanese positions in Marshall, Mariana, and Palau Islands in the central Pacific

1944, March, first African-American officers commissioned in U.S. Navy

June, U.S. Navy supports invasion of Normandy

The Nimitz-class aircraft carrier USS *Ronald Reagan* (CVN-76) was scheduled for launch at Newport News Shipbuilding of Newport News, Virginia, in 2002, 80 years after the commissioning of the U.S. Navy's first aircraft carrier. One of nine 1,040-foot ships of this largest class of nuclear-powered carriers, the *Reagan* represents the U.S. Navy's international role in maintaining America's forward presence on the world's sea-lanes. To operate the ship and its air wing of 72 aircraft requires a combined crew of nearly 6,000 men and women. Its four-acre landing deck is used by jet fighters, bombers, electronic counter-warfare planes, propeller-driven early warning aircraft with their radar domes, antisubmarine warfare and in-flight refueling jets, and antisubmarine warfare helicopters. Although designed in the 1960s to engage in superpower conflict with the Soviet Union during the Cold War, the Nimitz-class carriers and their associated battle groups are prepared for situations ranging from evacuating victims of natural disasters to protecting vital sea-lanes and fighting the small-scale, inshore conflicts that are likely to characterize war in the future. With these duties, U.S. Navy aircraft carriers will remain America's principal representatives on the high seas far into the twenty-first century. (Mystic Seaport, 98.96; Judy Beisler photo)

the aircraft carrier quickly became the capital ship of the Pacific war. At the Battle of the Coral Sea in May 1942, Japanese and American carrier task forces fought a two day aerial battle, never coming within visual range of one another on the sea.

The other significant naval engagements at Midway and off Guadalcanal in 1942, and in the Philippine Sea and at Leyte Gulf in 1944, were won by U.S. naval air power. Under the sea, the 220 U.S. submarines that operated during the war in the Pacific dominated the sea-lanes of that ocean even more successfully than did German U-boats that stalked the Atlantic sea-lanes. Despite more than 20 percent casualties among U.S. submarines and crews, American submarines sank one-third of the Japanese Imperial Navy and more than 1,000 merchant ships, severely limiting Japan's ability to support and supply its forces.

By the end of the war in 1945, the U.S. Navy was the world's largest, with 1,137 combat ships, thousands of landing craft and smaller vessels, and 3,400,000 men and women in uniform. Women filled many clerical positions as members of the WAVES (Women Accepted for Volunteer Emergency Service). African Americans, whose naval role had declined markedly since the Civil War, were accepted for positions on fighting ships by the end of the war and, for the first time, a few African Americans were commissioned as officers.

In Korea, in Vietnam, in the Gulf War of 1991, and in smaller actions right up to the NATO mission in Yugoslavia in 1999, the U.S. Navy has played a role with fire power, aircraft and missile attacks, and coastal patrols. From the 1950s to 1990, the navy was a prominent deterrent force during the "Cold War" with the Soviet Union. The subma-

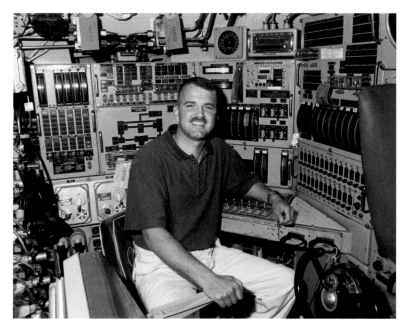

On board the Los Angeles-class fast attack submarine USS *Pittsburgh* (SSN-720), Petty Officer Joe Mikolajczak sits at one of the positions at the ship control station while off duty. When the submarine is underway, the helmsman, planesman, diving officer, and chief of the watch occupy this area and control the ship's movements. Carrying 13 officers and 120 crew, these 362-foot vessels patrol beneath the world's oceans on six-month deployments. The navy also operates larger Ohio-class ballistic missile submarines and a few new high-performance Seawolf attack submarines. Although they were designed to counter the nuclear threat of the Soviet Union, U.S. Navy nuclear submarines still have numerous roles and missions in the world since the end of the Cold War. From protecting aircraft carrier battle groups to launching missiles in warfare, from rescue operations to performing secret missions alongshore, quiet, fast, deep-diving nuclear submarines have become essential parts of the U.S. Navy fleet. (Mystic Seaport, Judy Beisler photo)

1944, June, aerial Battle of the Philippine Sea results in U.S. naval victory

23-25 October, naval Battle of Leyte Gulf in Philippines results in destruction of most of Japanese fleet

1945, February-March, U.S. Navy and Marines capture Iwo Jima

April-June, U.S. Army and Navy capture Okinawa

2 September, Japanese surrender on deck of USS *Missouri* in Tokyo Bay

September, at end of World War II, U.S. Navy includes 1,137 combat ships, 2,783 landing craft, thousands of smaller vessels, and 3,400,000 men and women

1949, first African-American midshipman, Wesley A. Brown, graduates from U.S. Naval Academy

April, North Atlantic Treaty Organization (NATO) established to coordinate U.S. and European military efforts, including naval operations

1950, September, as North Korean forces push south, U.S. amphibious assault at Inchon turns back the invasion, but after Chinese troops enter war it continues for three years, with naval air and coastal bombardment

1954, submarine USS *Nautilus*, first nuclear-powered vessel, launched at Groton, Connecticut

1958, August, USS *Nautilus* passes from Pacific to Atlantic under polar icecap, becoming first ship to reach the North Pole

1960, USS *George Washington* successfully fires Polaris missile, establishing possibility of nuclear-armed submarine force

1960-90, during the "Cold War" against the Soviet Union, U.S. nuclear-powered and nuclear-armed submarines provide the unseen threat of "mutual assured destruction" that helps prevent world war

1961, 5 May, U.S. Navy Lieutenant Commander Alan B. Shepard becomes first American in space on board *Freedom 7*

1962, October, to force removal of Soviet nuclear missiles from Cuba, U.S. Navy blockades the island, and the U.S. and Soviet Union come close to war

1964, after North Vietnamese fire on U.S. Navy vessels in the Gulf of Tonkin, U.S. escalates military effort in Vietnam, including naval air assaults, coastal bombardment, and patrols in Mekong River Delta

1971, Samuel L. Gravely, Jr., becomes first African-American Admiral in the U.S. Navy

1976, first women cadets admitted to U.S. Naval Academy

1978, women first assigned to duty on U.S. Navy ships (having long served on hospital ships)

1985, during Cold War military expansion, navy approaches 600-ship fleet

1990, end of Cold War leads to U.S. Navy force reductions and review of the navy's role

With the impressive size and complexity of modern U.S. Navy ships, it is easy to forget that they are still operated by human beings: as many as 6,000 on an aircraft carrier or 130 on a nuclear submarine. For many of these sailors, men and women alike, families wait ashore during overseas deployments that can last for six months at a time. When Petty Officer Joe Mikolajczak returned home in July 1999 his family met him with smiles and tears of joy in a greeting that symbolized the sacrifices of mariners and their families. (Claire White-Peterson photo)

rine USS *Nautilus*, the world's first nuclear-powered ship, introduced this capability, even as it explored new realms, becoming the first ship to reach the North Pole when it made a passage under the polar icecap in 1958. Beginning with the USS *George Washington* in 1960, ballistic missile submarines posed the threat of assured destruction to discourage Soviet aggression.

At the end of the twentieth century, the U.S. Navy is in the process of redefining its role and mission in a world without a major opponent but with many small conflicts.

52

A smaller, flexible, highly technological force emphasizing air and submarine power, armed with highly accurate missiles and operated by a cross-section of the American population, appears to be the U.S. Navy's shape for the twenty-first century. Although the U.S. Navy "sailor" of the modern era may be a female pilot, a computer analyst, or an electronics technician, they continue to observe the proud heritage of more than 200 years of naval seafaring.

> *... Yes, it is good to battle, and good to be strong and free,*
> *To carry the hearts of the people to the uttermost ends of the sea,*
> *To see the day steal up the bay where the enemy lies in wait,*
> *To run your ship to the harbor's lip and sink her across the strait:—*
> *But better the golden evening when the ships round heads for home,*
> *and the long gray miles slip swiftly past in a swirl of seething foam,*
> *And the people wait at the haven's gate to greet the men who win!*
> *Thank God for peace! Thank God for peace, when the great gray*
> *   ships come in!*

Guy Wetmore Carryl, *"When the Great Gray Ships Come In"* (1898)

1991, U.S. Navy provides aircraft and missile attack on Iraq during Gulf War

1997, U.S. Navy numbers 347 ships and 340,000 men and women

1999, U.S. Navy aircraft and submarines participate in NATO bombardment of Yugoslavia

Part Five

ENJOYING THE WATER

Oceans, lakes, and rivers are not just avenues of commerce or theaters of warfare. They are arenas of sport, and America's favorite destinations for relaxation and fun.

Americans have not always had the time, money, or inclination to go to sea for the fun of it. But in the last century and a half, millions of men, women, and children have taken to boating, sailing, heading to the beach, or shipping out on a cruise.

What's your idea of fun on the water? Do you push yourself and your boat to the limit in competition, or do you slip away in search of peace and quiet?

Do you paddle out in an old wooden canoe, load your fishing gear into a trusty aluminum motorboat, or sail away in a fiberglass day-sailer? Come aboard now and see how strong these maritime traditions remain, and how many different ways Americans have found to enjoy themselves on our lakes, rivers, and at sea.

More than any other environment on earth, water has become synonymous with recreation. We now think of boating or the beach when we think of the sea, but it has not always been so. Although wealthy colonists in the 1600s and 1700s might copy wealthy Europeans in having small vessels in which they could escape the summer heat of the land, most Americans had little time for recreation. The water was a place of work, and though professional boatmen might race each other or crews from other maritime powers, sometimes in front of betting spectators, the average American looked at the water more with fear than with longing. Some used it as a place of productive leisure, catching fish or gathering shellfish, but the beach was considered a wasteland, not a playground.

In America, the shift to waterside recreation came in the 1800s, as cities increased in size, and as life in them became more regimented and confining. The regular hours of industrial labor, as well as the independence of skilled artisans, normally allowed at least half of

Illustration on page 54: Cruising the "sunlane" to Europe in 1960 may not have been the most popular vacation experience, but it represented the shift in ocean liner use from intercontinental travel to recreational cruising as jet aircraft took over the bulk of long-distance travel. After a decline that saw most of the grand liners retired, a new generation of opulent ships designed for cruising now carries millions of passengers out of American ports each year around the Caribbean, along the Pacific coast, and in the Hawai'ian Islands. (Mystic Seaport, 96.142.9, Jennifer M. Stich photo)

Saturday for recreation, and the pressures of urban life encouraged people to seek diversion. The steam engine, which might be powering their productivity at work, also gave them access to a larger environment. Steamboats, and later railroads, linked coastal cities, such as Boston, New York, or Philadelphia, with picnic grounds or beaches that would soon become resorts.

The urban environment also led to the growth of organized sports for both participants and spectators. Boat clubs gave people of limited means a way to get on the water for leisure or competition, and yacht clubs offered wealthier individuals both camaraderie and competition through organized activities. By the 1850s both of these forms of organized boating had become well established, as represented by the formation of the Detroit Boat Club in 1839 and the New York Yacht Club in 1844. Yachting and boating took on national significance with the victory of the New York Yacht Club's schooner *America* in an 1851 race against the best British yachts during an exposition of international progress, and the 1852 rowing race between boats representing Harvard and Yale, which was the first intercollegiate sporting event.

Long before the Civil War, Newport, Rhode Island, had begun to attract wealthy Southern families as a healthy seaside alternative to hot, disease-prone Southern cities in summer. Beaches and resorts were established in places like Coney Island, New York, and Atlantic City, New Jersey, where urban residents could escape for even a day. Boardinghouses and rustic hotels were added to house those whose employment included an actual vacation. Amusements and games of chance added a carnival atmosphere to the beach experience at a time when swimming was only beginning to be popular and a sun tan was associated with outdoor laborers. Although beach activities were informal in comparison with daily life, beach dress remained formal, with long skirts and often veils for women, and swimming suits were designed to disguise the body within.

With the expansion of railroad and steamboat lines, more remote areas, such as the Gulf Coast, the Great Lakes, Cape Cod, the mountains and lakes of upstate New York, and the Maine coast and lakes were opened to recreation. Large and small tourist hotels were built, diversifying the local economy while offering new experiences for vacationers. In many coastal or lakefront areas groups built summer colonies. Sometimes families from the same inland town built cottages at the shore together. The community of summer cottages at Oak Bluffs on the island of Martha's Vineyard grew out of a Methodist summer encampment, and religious revivals or retreats led to other resorts as well. Recreational fishing attracted individuals who built camps or established fishing clubs in other areas, such as the island of Cuttyhunk, Massachusetts, the many lakes in the Rangeley region of Maine and the Adirondack Mountains of New York, or Key West, Florida. With the strengthening of "Jim Crow" laws that restricted African Americans from general travel, food, and lodging after the 1880s, blacks were forced to establish separate resorts, including several communities along the Carolina coast near Charleston. By 1900 summer resorts had become national institutions.

While waterside recreation expanded greatly in the decades after the Civil War, so too did on-the-water forms of recreation. Recreation and national prestige came together in the ongoing competition for the America's Cup, the trophy won by the schooner-yacht *America* in 1851. As holder of the trophy, the New York Yacht Club set up rules for challenges, and from 1870 to 1903 British or Canadian challengers vied for the cup against American defenders every three or four years. The first defense, in 1870, pitted the best schooners of the New York Yacht Club against a lone challenger. Thereafter, a single yacht was chosen through competition to defend the cup against a challenging vessel, which had to come to America under sail to participate. In the 1880s competition moved from schooners to a new generation of advanced sloops designed by professional naval architects. By the 1890s these vessels were built of steel or bronze, and they carried crews of 60 or more to handle their great expanses of sail. The largest, the American sloop *Reliance* of 1903, was more than 140 feet long.

The America's Cup and most large yacht club racing was a spectator sport conducted with large boats operated by professional captains and crews. At the other extreme, small sailing yachts were adapted from workboat designs for racing, cruising, or day-sailing by individuals. In busy ports like New York, Philadelphia, and New Orleans, watermen and amateurs formed clubs to race the extreme boats of their regions—the wide, shallow, heavily rigged sandbaggers with moveable ballast in New York and New Orleans; small, light, heavily rigged hikers and tuckups in Philadelphia; log canoes on Chesapeake Bay; and whaleboats on San Francisco Bay. Until industrial development drove this kind of recreation off the waterfront, boat racing was a popular spectator sport for urban residents.

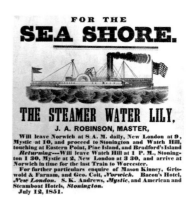

FOR THE SEA SHORE.

THE STEAMER WATER LILY,

J. A. ROBINSON, MASTER,

Will leave Norwich at 8 A. M. daily, New London at 9, Mystic at 10, and proceed to Stonington and Watch Hill, touching at Eastern Point, Pine Island, and Bradford's Island *Returning*---Will leave Watch Hill at 1 P. M., Stonington 1 30, Mystic at 2, New London at 3 30, and arrive at Norwich in time for the last Train to Worcester.
For further particulars enquire of Mason Kinney, Griswold & Farnam, and Geo. Colt, *Norwich.* Bacon's Hotel, *New London.* S. K. Andrews, *Mystic,* and American and Steamboat Hotels, *Stonington.*
July 12, 1851.

The steamboat provided access to the shore for inland residents, opening up new recreational possibilities. A steamboat ride itself could be a pleasure trip, taking people out of their accustomed routines. Or it could take them to the nearby resorts that catered to both day and overnight visitors. For residents of industrial Norwich, Connecticut, the *Water Lily*'s 25-mile excursion route, which took about three hours by water, would have taken all day by land. (Mystic Seaport, 54.1384)

1829, Coney Island, Brooklyn, begins as a seaside resort with one small hotel. With the addition of a bathhouse and pavilion in 1844, the introduction of railroad service in 1874, and the construction of piers and amusement parks through the 1890s, it would become one of the leading seaside resorts, with as many as 100,000 visitors a day

1839, Detroit Boat Club established as first American boating club

1844, New York Yacht Club established as first American yacht club

1847, representing the importance of food to recreation, Rocky Point Park established in Rhode Island, becoming famous for its "shore dinners" of clams. In other regions, lobsters, oysters, or other local resources became the focus of these recreational feasts

Launched at Mystic, Connecticut, in 1866, the schooner yacht *Dauntless* was owned by the flamboyant yachtsman and newspaper editor James Gordon Bennett, Jr., from 1867 to 1878. As depicted in this spirited oil painting by James E. Buttersworth, Bennett often raced his schooner, participating in the first defense of the America's Cup in 1870 and in many New York Yacht Club races. He and his professional crew also sailed the 116-foot schooner to Europe several times. (Mystic Seaport, 76.172)

In the 1870s, as yachting expanded, the "Corinthian movement" turned boat owners into boat sailers and expanded the fleet of sailboats and yacht clubs, such as the Seawanhaka Yacht Club on Long Island, the International Yacht Club of Detroit, and the St. Augustine Yacht Club in Florida. This form of sailing was a participatory sport; indeed, professional watermen were prohibited from competing in amateur races. To emphasize skill over individual vessel design, the yacht clubs that organized sailboat racing began to sponsor one-design classes of similar boats. The Star class, designed in 1911, was the first truly international class of small racing sailboat. Sailed on both salt and fresh water, the Star remains one of the most competitive classes.

With the expansion of wealth and leisure during the industrial age after the Civil War, more individuals owned large yachts, and the exploits of some, like publisher James Gordon Bennett, Jr., with his schooner *Dauntless* and later steam yachts, became news. By the 1880s, grand steam yachts had become movable mansions, like J.P. Morgan's *Corsair*s, able to take their owners and guests on extended trips along the coast or even across the ocean. They became symbols of American industrial power, both in the fortunes that underwrote them and in the very technology that created and operated them.

Based on the writings of the Scottish adventurer John "Rob Roy" MacGregor, Native American paddling boats also were adapted for recreation. MacGregor's writings about his solo cruising in a double-paddle wooden canoe in the 1860s inspired many who were used to rowing, facing backwards, to turn around and paddle, facing forward. The establishment of local canoe clubs across the nation, as well as the American Canoe Association in 1880, attested to the popularity of the recreational canoe. "Canoes" came in many forms, produced by a new recreational industry. Inuit canoes of the Arctic inspired wooden kayak-style canoes like MacGregor's. Amateurs made notable journeys in them, down the Mississippi River, through the lakes, or along the coast, like Mr. and Mrs. Henry A. Wise Wood, who canoed from Massachusetts to Prince Edward Island in 1908. Out of these boats grew a style of decked sailing canoe, with centerboard and hiking plank, that tested the extremes of sailing in highly competitive international races. Native birchbark canoes of the Northeast inspired wood-canvas canoes for work and recreation typified by those built in many shops in Maine, including what came to be known as the Old Town Canoe Company.

Tourists and "sports" heading to the mountains and lakes of upstate New York and Maine provided a new opportunity for local inhabitants to act as hunting and fishing guides. They adapted local boats for these recreational uses, including the distinctive Adirondack guideboat and St. Lawrence River skiff of New York and the Rangeley boat of Maine. Tourists and "day-trippers" who wanted to do it themselves patronized boat liveries for a few hours of enjoyment on the water, further encouraging boat and canoe builders.

Those of lesser means who did not wish to row or sail or paddle might hire an engineer to operate a small steam engine in an open launch, or could use the new naphtha engine, based on the expansive properties of this volatile liquid, to drive a boat. By the 1890s the gasoline engine had been perfected for use in boats, and this brought more people onto the water for pleasure. By 1903, boatbuilders were building more powerboats than sailboats. Cameron Waterman built the first production portable engine, which he named the outboard, in 1907, two years before Ole Evinrude developed his outboard and, with his wife's management skills, captured the market, proclaiming: "Don't row, throw the oars away! Use an Evinrude motor."

With more leisure time, a more regular income, and greater access to the water through rail and automobile transportation, Americans bought even more canoes, motorboats, and small sailboats. The number of

The most opulent form of yachting was traveling in a steam yacht outfitted with many of the features of a mansion ashore. After selling their controlling shares in the trust that produced tin-plate, W.B. Leeds and his partner ordered matching steam yachts from the noted designer Clinton Crane. Leeds made so many alterations to the plans and added so many luxurious appointments that Crane feared the yacht would be a failure. Launched in 1902, 262-foot steel-hulled *Noma* pleased Leeds and was faster than her designer expected. After eight years of cruising and racing, Leeds sold his vessel to John Jacob Astor, whose family kept the yacht even after Astor died on the *Titanic*. (Mystic Seaport, 66.336; Judy Beisler photo)

1890s, gasoline engine perfected as safer alternative to steam engines or naphtha engines in small recreational boats

1903, 144-foot America's Cup defender *Reliance*, the largest sloop-rigged vessel ever built, defeats Sir Thomas Lipton's *Shamrock III*

1904, Gold Cup speedboat races established as national test of powerboat speed by American Powerboat Association

1907, principles of the water-cooled outboard motor perfected by Cameron Waterman, two years before Ole Evinrude begins producing his highly successful outboard

1911, introduction of the Star-class sloop, which for decades was the leading international one-design racing sailboat

1915, *Disturber IV*, first boat to travel faster than 60 miles per hour

U.S. Power Squadrons incorporated to offer boat safety and handling classes to the public

1917-19, as part of the Naval Reserves during World War I, yachtsmen and boaters contribute their maritime skills during time of war

1921, reestablishment of long-distance Chicago-to-Mackinac Race for sailboats on Lake Michigan (first sailed in 1898)

1922, Chris Smith & Sons Boat Company, the forerunner of Chris-Craft, founded in Michigan as one of the production boat companies established alongside the automobile industry. With their extremely popular 26-foot runabout, the company would control 15 percent of the pleasureboat market by 1929

1923, establishment of New London (later Newport)-to-Bermuda Race and reestablishment of Los Angeles-to-Honolulu Transpacific Race (first sailed in 1906) continues popularity of long-distance ocean racing

1924, Cruising Club of America founded by long-distance ocean sailors

1931, launch of 408-foot *Savarona III*, the largest American yacht ever built

1932, Gar Wood's hydroplane *Miss America X*, defending the British International Cup for Motorboats (the Harmsworth Trophy), records a run of 124 miles per hour

Mountain lakes in Maine, New York, and elsewhere had become popular recreation destinations by the 1870s. Here even people of moderate means could get a rustic break from city life. At the Lake View House, at Bolton Landing on New York's Lake George, boating was clearly a popular form of recreation for both men and women. S.R. Stoddard photographed this tranquil scene in 1889. (Mystic Seaport, 85.60.1)

recreational boats grew from about 15,000 in 1904 to 400,000 in 1914, to more than 8,000,000 in 1994.

As recreational boating grew, it could support a popular press. *The Rudder*, established in 1890, was the first successful American boating magazine which, through its editor, the avid boatman Thomas Fleming Day, published articles on boating experiences as well as practical instructions for boatowners and product and design sections. Other magazines, such as *Motor Boat*, launched in 1904, and *Yachting*, which made its debut in 1907, informed readers about boating and promoted boating products through advertising. As the boating industry expanded to profit from popular demand for boating products, the boating trade show was introduced in 1905 with the establishment of the New York Boat Show.

Through the 1920s sailing continued its popularity, with an increase in the number of one-design classes for small-boat sailing. With the decline of commercial sailing vessels, adventurers who wanted to experience life under sail had to make their own voyages. Some headed off to discover the South Pacific, often aboard reconditioned watercraft. The Cruising Club of America, founded in 1924 with the motto "nowhere is too far," created a network to provide information, promote design improvements, and enhance the skills of those who wanted to

Ole Evinrude, who arrived in Wisconsin from Norway at age five, was working as a machinist when a long row on a summer day in 1905 got him thinking about other ways to power a small boat. Cameron Waterman had introduced a practical outboard motor in 1906, and Evinrude came up with a similar idea. Working with his wife Bess, Evinrude sold his first outboard in 1909 and filed for a patent in 1910. Evinrude outboards quickly became a popular success as people heeded Bess Evinrude's advertisement: "Don't row, throw the oars away! Use an Evinrude motor." Evinrude sold his share in the company in 1914, founding the Elto (Evinrude light twin outboard) Company in 1920 to produce aluminum motors. The firms were merged in 1929 as part of the Outboard Motors Corporation (OMC), producing models for the full range of recreational users. When advertising the half-horsepower Elto Cub, introduced in 1940, the company depicted the range of users who had quit rowing to use an Evinrude. (Mystic Seaport, 97.104.21)

make long passages or explore remote regions of the sea. Racing sailors could also challenge themselves with distance races from southern New England to Bermuda, from Chicago to Mackinac, from California to Hawai'i, or across the Atlantic, all of which were revived in the 1920s.

1942-45, serving in the Naval and Coast Guard Reserves during World War II, yachtsmen and boaters contribute their maritime skills during time of war

1947, introduction of fiberglass recreational boats, including the Winner 10-foot dinghy, the Beetle Cat in 1948, and the Dyer Dhow in 1949

1948, the Alcort Sailfish introduces sailing board boats, followed later by their Sunfish

1950s, Ray Hunt introduces the shapes of modern motorboats, designing the Boston Whaler and the deep-V hull characteristic of powerboats today, which would be powered by the inboard-outboard "Z drive" after 1960

1961, Cape Cod National Seashore established by Congress as part of National Park Service to preserve shoreside and provide public access; other national seashores and lakeshores established later on all coasts

1968, expanding popularity of personal watercraft leads to development of the Windsurfer, followed by the Laser in 1970 and of multihull boats like the Hobie Cat

National Wild and Scenic Rivers System established by Congress to preserve undeveloped waterways for recreational access and conservation

1970s, popular rediscovery of traditional watercraft design and wooden construction, largely influenced by boatbuilder and historian John Gardner

Thomas Fleming Day (1861-1927), the son of a British scientist, came to New York as a child and worked for a marine hardware firm and as a boat salesman based in Upstate New York before becoming the founding editor of the first American boating magazine, *The Rudder*, in 1890. An avid boatman despite his frail health, he was passionate about all things maritime. A poet and great companion, Day was above all a philosopher of the sea who believed in making boats accessible to everyone so that they might learn "presence of mind" at the helm of a boat. To encourage amateur builders and sailors he designed and published small boat plans in *The Rudder*. To prove the utility of his small ocean cruising design, *Sea Bird*, he sailed the 26-foot boat across the Atlantic in 1911. The following year he made the first transatlantic crossing by gasoline engine, with a crew of three in the motorboat *Detroit*. (Mystic Seaport, 96.96.669)

Through the Great Depression of the 1930s, the America's Cup competition was revived with the adoption of the one-design J-Class sloop. In 1930, 1934, and 1937 these grand and glamorous racing machines served as a focus of yachting patriotism in a time when few could afford the extravagance of high-style yachting. Competition was not resumed until 1958. Sailing 12-Meter sloops, U.S. yachtsmen defended the America's Cup until 1983, when an Australian boat won. Competition continues.

Links between the automobile industry and powerboat industry had become even stronger by the 1920s. Light, high-performance engines derived from automobile and World War I aircraft engines made motorboats ever lighter and faster. International competition for the Harmsworth Trophy in hydroplanes designed to skim across the water attracted huge crowds to watch boats approach and exceed 100 miles per hour. Racers like Gar Wood and Chris Smith capitalized on their popularity to establish production boat companies, building stock models for recreational boaters. Located near the automobile industry in the Midwest, companies like Chris Smith's Chris-Craft, founded in 1922, used some of the same techniques to make motorboating as easy as owning a car. By the late 1920s Chris-Craft controlled more than 15 percent of the market for recreational boats. Those who wanted a somewhat larger cabin yacht might buy one of the stock cruisers built on the East Coast by Elco, while those who wanted to go fast might try a Hickman Sea Sled, built in Mystic, Connecticut, to a model similar to today's Boston Whaler.

Florida had been a destination for the wealthy since the 1890s, but in the 1920s middle-class mobility opened more of the coast to residential and recreational development. Around several coastal urban areas, including New York, Detroit, and Chicago, the wealthy built waterside estates, sometimes traveling to work in the city aboard large, fast powerboats nicknamed "commuters." Those who could not escape city life could at least visit an increasing number of public beaches, and even municipal swimming pools, to have a water experience. Public beaches and state parks became more important as residential and resort development made water access increasingly limited. Beginning with the Cape Cod National Seashore in 1961, the federal government has controlled development and provided access to shorefront on all four coasts. The National Wild and Scenic Rivers system, established in 1968, addresses similar issues on undeveloped waterways.

World Wars I and II were not times of recreation, yet recreational boaters played a part. In both wars, recreational sailers joined the U.S. Naval Reserve as the navy expanded, providing an immediate pool of experienced officers for naval vessels. The U.S. Coast Guard's "Hooligan Navy" employed former yachts and yachtsmen to patrol much of the U.S. East Coast between 1942 and 1945, on watch for the German U-boats that preyed on merchant shipping. Yacht yards converted to constructing wooden minesweepers, PT-boats, and patrol and utility craft, bringing many retired wooden boatbuilders out of retirement for a last flurry of large wooden boat construction. After the war, recreational boatbuilding would benefit from wartime developments in aluminum, plywood, and fiberglass construction.

Through the 1900s, as the water became a place of recreation for everyone, some boat designers looked beyond the sea to find inspiration for new designs. The interplay between land, air, and water is represented by the Evinrude Lark, a 1956 fiberglass boat designed by Brooks Stevens with elements taken from aircraft and the most stylish automobiles of the day. As they have for 100 years, boat and motor manufacturers often employed a model in a stylish bathing suit to entice male buyers. (© Mystic Seaport, Rosenfeld Collection, Mystic, Connecticut)

The Amphi-Craft trailer is designed to minimize the lifting and simplify the fastening required to secure this boat for transportation.

All spars, rigging and gear can be safely and easily secured inside the hull beneath the canvas tarpaulin which covers the open cockpit when the boat is on the trailer.

The boat was designed for power as well as sail, and is fitted with a re-enforced transom to take an outboard motor. It makes it adaptable for fishing, hunting, camping and picnicking on inland or seacoast waters. A light-weight hooded outboard motor is furnished as an extra.

The Amphi-Craft has a centerboard and an adjustable rudder which permits its use in shallow as well as deeper waters.

Oars are conveni[ently] stored for those who [prefer] the exhilaration of row[ing] or for auxiliary powe[r when] calm.

Herreshoff **AMPHI-CRAFT**

This recent Herreshoff creation adds a new thrill to your week-ends, opens up thousands of miles of water-ways hitherto inaccessible, and gives those who must live in the city a chance to vagabond at will on their holidays, at such yachting centers as Newport, Lake Placid, or to fish from secluded mountain streams; suitable for hunting, ideal for fishing, the camper or picnicker will find countless recreational and practical uses for this all-purpose boat.

Page Thirty-eight

The Amphi-Craft was designed in the 1930s as the ultimate in portable rowing, sailing, or outboard-powered boats. Reflecting the importance of the automobile in getting people to the water, the Amphi-Craft came with a trailer. This 13-foot boat was designed by Sidney Herreshoff and built at the Herreshoff Manufacturing Company, which was well known for the large yachts and highly engineered America's Cup defenders designed by Sidney's father, Nathanael Greene Herreshoff. This advertisement appeared in the company's 1935 catalog, *Yachts by Herreshoff*. (Mystic Seaport, G.W. Blunt White Library)

1983, with the defeat of the U.S. America's Cup defender, the 12-meter sloop *Liberty*, by the Australian challenger *Australia II*, the oldest symbol of international sport leaves U.S. hands for the first time in 133 years

1992, with the proliferation of foreign-flag cruise ships sailing from U.S. ports, Congress passes the Cruise Ship Competitiveness Act, permitting gambling on U.S.-flag vessels and otherwise encouraging cruising on U.S.-registered vessels

1995, in a great return to sea travel, nearly 5,000,000 Americans book passage on cruise ships operated by Disney, Carnival Cruise Lines (including Cunard and Holland-America), and others

Showing off the latest in fashionable beach wear, a group gathers at the water's edge at Long Branch, New Jersey, 31 July 1929. It is still three months before the stock market crash that would announce the Great Depression, and these beachgoers are ready to enjoy themselves with a refreshing swim or simply lounging on the sand. Notice the inflatable toys. Long Branch had been a popular resort since before Winslow Homer painted there in the 1870s, and it remains so 70 years after this photograph. (Negative 35841, © Mystic Seaport, Rosenfeld Collection)

1997, Americans own approximately 12,309,724 boats, the 5 leading states—Michigan, California, Florida, Minnesota, and Texas—accounting for 3,987,107

With the expansion of southern California, a year-round athletic beach culture began to flourish. Bodybuilding and volleyball were part of this, as was the Hawai'ian sport of surfing. Bathing suits now revealed rather than concealed their wearers. Popularized through film and television during the 1950s and 1960s, these activities spread across the country. Beginning with the introduction of Alcort's Sailfish in 1948, beach boats combined elements of surfing and sailing. In the late 1960s the highly popular Laser and Windsurfer emphasized the concept's origins in the small sailboat and the surfboard. On the West Coast, Hobie Alter combined elements of the Hawai'ian outrigger with fiberglass and aluminum to produce a high-performance catamaran that became a popular beach boat on all coasts. The beach boats accommodate users with a wide range of skills, opening up sailing to many who might not otherwise enjoy it.

The introduction of fiberglass and of lighter, more powerful outboard motors influenced powerboat design as well. The innovative designer Ray Hunt brought out the sea sled-like Boston Whaler in the 1950s. In 1957 he introduced the deep -V hull, which lifts the bow and runs very efficiently at high speed. Bertram Yachts began offering production models in the 1960s, and the hull form

64

is now almost universal among open-water powerboats. The inboard-outboard, or "Z-drive," introduced in 1960, was the ideal power train for this hull form. By the 1990s, the maritime equivalent of the motorcycle or snowmobile was available in the form of the extremely popular jet-ski, which uses a water pump rather than a propeller. With all of this variety, the most common powerboat today appears to be the "bass boat," used for recreational fishing on lakes, rivers, and sheltered waters around the country. Like beach boats, these powerboats are portable, relatively inexpensive, and adaptable for uses from sightseeing to fishing to waterskiing.

In recent decades, fiberglass and plastic have given new life to the varieties of native canoes and kayaks, which have become extremely popular personal watercraft. Even as these materials took over the boating industry, others have found great satisfaction in creating both traditional and modern designs in the traditional boatbuilder's material: wood.

Until the late 1950s the ship was the principal method of traveling across oceans. Special excursions had been offered since the mid-1800s, and many travelers used ships to get to their sightseeing destinations, but for most the shipboard side of travel was a means to an end. However, ever since air travel superseded long-distance water travel, the novelty of cruising at sea—especially the Caribbean in winter and Alaskan waters in summer—or on the rivers has captured the public imagination. Emphasizing luxury and all forms of leisure gratification for millions of passengers each year, cruising has turned the sea into a greater playground than ever. The largest cruise ships, 900 feet long and accommodating 2,600 passengers, are larger than the *Titanic* and the other great ocean liners of the past. Although most of the ships are registered in other countries and fly foreign flags to avoid high costs of U.S. ship operation, cruise ships have added a whole new dimension to the port of Miami. Cruising, and vacationing by airline, have altered the economies of the Caribbean islands, including the U.S. possessions of Puerto Rico and the Virgin Islands, to emphasize tourism.

It is no wonder that we look to the sea for recreation. Whether boating or beaching, this contact with the sea takes us out of our routines, offering the possibility of adventure, romance, accomplishment, or simple good fun.

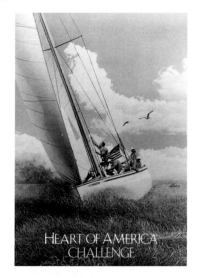

HEART OF AMERICA CHALLENGE

Although limited to an elite group of large yacht sailors, the America's Cup competition became a public event that combined recreation with national pride during 25 challenges between 1870 and 1983. After *Australia II* won the America's Cup with an innovative winged keel in 1983, Americans became challengers in this oldest continuous sporting event. Among the 13 competitors aiming to win the cup from Australia in 1987 was *Heart of America*, which emphasized its ties to the U.S. heartland in this graphic appeal for financial support. Technology was as important as sailing skill in these 12-Meter-Class sloops, as skipper Buddy Melges demonstrated when he added a new winged keel to increase his boat's performance. It was *Stars & Stripes*, however, that reclaimed the cup. Competition had a Pacific Ocean orientation through the 1990s, sailed by representatives of San Diego, Australia, and New Zealand, largely underwritten by corporate rather than private wealth. (Mystic Seaport, 88.367)

WICO BRAND TUNA

CALIFORNIA

WICO BRAND TUNA

U.S. SERIAL

PACKED IN S.
DELICIOUS
SALADS.
READY TO SE

DISTRIBUTED BY
WESTERN IMPORT CO.
SAN FRANCISCO CAL.

CAPE BRAND

Fresh
Columbia River

SALMON

CAPE BRAND

SALMON

Carnation BRAND BARATARIA

SHRIMP

PACKED BY G.W. DUNBAR'S SONS,
BRANCH
DUNBARS, LOPEZ & DUKATE CO.,
NEW ORLEANS, LA–BILOXI, MISS.

GUARANTEED BY DUNBARS, LOPEZ & DUKATE CO.,
UNDER FOOD AND DRUGS ACT, JUNE 30TH, 1906.
SERIAL No. A14-46.

CARNATION BRAND

SHRIMP

WALLE & CO., LTD., N.O. LA.

CO-OPERATORS'

SPRING CATCH

BEST

ROYAL CHINOOK

SALMON

MEDIUM RED SALMON

COHO SALMON

LIGHTLY SALTED

SLEDGE BRAND
PACKED BY

ALASKA PACKERS ASSOCIATION, San Francisco.

REG. U. S. PAT. OFF.
LIGHTLY SALTED

SLEDGE BRAND COHO SALMON

Part Six

GATHERING RESOURCES FROM THE SEA

For thousands of years the inhabitants of North America have ventured onto the water to hunt fish, whales, and seals; to gather shellfish and plants; to cultivate marine life; to recover salt, minerals, and petroleum; and even to harness the power of moving water. Americans today still depend on the sea's many essential resources.

The range of American "fishermen" represents the breadth of American culture: Native-American "first people," descendants of Europeans, Africans, and Asians, male and female. Their work, pursued largely beyond our sight and often at great risk, has shaped their lives in fundamental ways, just as it nourishes ours.

The marine resources of the North American Continent once seemed unlimited. The continent's three saltwater coasts stretch for 8,000 miles, with 2,000 miles more along the Great Lakes and easily 5,000 miles of major rivers that drain much of the continent. Far beneath areas of the ocean bottom lie pockets of petroleum, the carbon residue of life forms that flourished in earlier seas tens of millions of years ago.

The continent's abundant rain- and snowfall finds its way to the sea through many river systems. The seaward rush of water itself is a potential resource for energy, for drinking water, and for water to irrigate farm fields.

These uses of the nation's rivers compete with the natural adaptation of many types of fish that live in the sea but reproduce in fresh water. Adult salmon in both the Atlantic and Pacific, and several species of the herring family in the Atlantic made their way far upstream to spawn in the freshwater streams of their birth. Blocking these waterways breaks the natural cycle.

Especially on the Atlantic and Gulf coasts, the rivers meet the sea in broad, shallow estuaries and bayous, where fresh and salt water mix. Here the flow of nutrients coming downstream and the in- and outwash of the tide provides ideal habitat for many species of shellfish, from clams and oysters to lobsters. These estuaries and the surrounding marshes are the nurseries

Developing the
Resources of the Sea:
A Chronology

ca. 10,000 BC, outwash from
receding ice sheet leaves ridges
on the exposed Atlantic coast
continental shelf, which are
flooded to become "banks"
as the sea rises at the end of
the Ice Age

Fish were essential resources
for Native Americans. This
carving from the Arctic depicts
a native, dressed in a suit of
skins, who has just caught a
salmon through the ice.
(Mystic Seaport, 64.1334;
Judy Beisler photo)

ca. 8,000 BC, Native Americans
in Columbia River basin begin to
depend on migrating salmon for
subsistence and trade, and as a
cultural symbol

Illustration on page 66: From
its development around 1840,
seafood canning became the
leading method of preserving
fish by 1940. Lobsters and oysters were among the first seafood
items canned. With the introduction of sardine and salmon
canning in the 1860s and tuna
canning around 1910 these fish
became the leading convenience
foods for workmen and others
seeking inexpensive protein
sources. To distinguish their
products, canning companies
produced colorfully distinctive
names and labels for their cans.
(Mystic Seaport, 99.69, 97.112.10,
99.36.2, 97.112.1, 99.72.1)

for a large volume of marine life. In addition, the continent's rivers and lakes contain natural populations of fresh-water fish.

Along the shallow continental shelf, where nutrients and sunlight mix, life forms ranging from single-celled plankton to marine mammals exist in an interdependent "food web." Especially fertile areas lie in the North Atlantic and North Pacific, where warm- and cold-water currents interact, stirring up the nutrients around the underwater ridges called banks. Some fish, such as the cod, graze these underwater ridges and plains in herds, while flatfish, such as halibut and flounder, normally lie in wait for their prey on the bottom.

Near the surface, mackerel, menhaden, and other schooling fish swarm up the East Coast in summer to spawn, while predatory fish like bluefish, striped bass, swordfish, and tuna lurk around the schools. Marine mammals from seals to whales also migrate seasonally alongshore and in the open sea. Sperm whales, the largest toothed whales, swim in groups called pods well offshore in all temperate oceans. Right whales, which have long, flexible strips of baleen in their mouths to strain their food from seawater, migrate alongshore. The similar bowhead lives in Arctic waters.

Native peoples began to use marine resources thousands of years before European settlers first arrived. Archaeological evidence indicates that residents of the Columbia River basin on the West Coast had made salmon a principal part of their culture nearly 10,000 years ago. Along the coast from present-day California to Alaska, the native cultures depended on marine products rather than agriculture, and they developed some of the richest societies in North America. Peoples of the Arctic were dependent on fish, seals, and whales for their survival, while natives on the East Coast settled along estuaries in summer to devour the shellfish and fin fish that were easy to catch in those sheltered waters. Farther north, native peoples also hunted whales near shore and gathered menhaden and other common schooling fish to fertilize their cornfields.

When the English sent John Cabot to explore the North Atlantic in 1497, he discovered the great population of codfish around Newfoundland. Cod was considered an ideal source of protein because it can be dried and preserved with salt. Within a few years, hundreds of European vessels were fishing those waters in summer. French, Spanish, and Portuguese fishermen pickled their cod on board, while English fishermen established "stages" on shore to salt and air-dry their fish before returning home. These fishing camps were the first European outposts in English America.

Although they looked down on the rough, unsettled, intemperate fishermen who pioneered the industry, the Pilgrims and Puritans viewed fish as a source of income. As the Reverend William Morrell expressed in his 1625 poem "New-England":

> *The costly cod doth march with his rich traine:*
> *With which the merchant doth much riches get:*
> *With which plantations richly may subsist,*
> *And pay their merchants debt and interest.*

European settlements in North America were intended to produce resources for their mother countries. Without precious metals or great agricultural potential, the New England colonies developed the natural products of timber and fish. Salted cod became a principal commodity of the Massachusetts Bay Colony's trade with England and southern Europe. By the mid-1700s, New England harbored a fleet of several hundred small vessels with perhaps 10,000 fishermen—who also split and salted the catch—and packers. Other coastal species of fish and shellfish were gathered for domestic consumption. Whale products also became important, first from the whales found along the Long Island and Cape Cod coast, then from those hunted offshore by the whalemen of Nantucket. After Nantucketers took the first sperm whale and discovered the quality of its oil and the use of its spermaceti to make fine candles, whaling became a growing New England industry.

The early settlers also recognized water as a resource in several forms. To power their mills for cutting wood and grinding grain they dammed waterways and channeled the water to turn mill wheels. In the 1800s engineers developed a more efficient type of mill wheel, the turbine, to power large mills. Water power remained the most important force in American industry until after the Civil War.

In another form of alchemy, salt from seawater became a commodity during the American Revolution, when European and Caribbean sources were cut off. By 1800 Cape Cod saltmakers used the sun to evaporate seawater in shallow troughs, producing a bushel of salt from 350 gallons of water. Until inland salt beds were tapped in the 1830s, evaporated sea salt was an important commodity.

The bloody hunt for marine mammals expanded in the

ca. 1000 AD, marine resources of the North Pacific support world's most sophisticated nonagricultural societies along coast from present-day Oregon to Alaska

ca. 1400, marine resources in Southern New England help support Native American population density on Nantucket Island equal to that of Northern Europe

1497, John Cabot brings back word of codfish resources discovered off Newfoundland

1502, European fishing fleets working in Newfoundland waters

1620, having landed in New England, Pilgrims plan to use fish as a trade commodity

ca. 1650, alongshore whale fishery established by European settlers on Long Island, New York, with assistance of Native American whalers

1712, first recorded capture of a sperm whale

ca. 1720, codfishermen of Marblehead and Gloucester, Massachusetts, begin to dominate New England commercial fisheries

ca. 1750, Rhode Islanders begin to manufacture candles from the waxy spermaceti of sperm whales

1762, New Haven, Connecticut, passes act to protect natural oyster beds

1783, U.S. fishing rights to waters off Newfoundland and Labrador and in Gulf of St. Lawrence recognized in Treaty of Paris ending American Revolution

1784, wooden codfish hung in Massachusetts House of Representatives "as a memorial of the importance of the cod fishery to the welfare of this Commonwealth"

ca. 1790, damming of Connecticut River and tributaries for industrial power shuts off access to most Atlantic salmon spawning grounds, nearly eliminating that fish in southern New England waters

1791, first American whaleships round Cape Horn and enter the Pacific Ocean

1793, U.S. Congress establishes system of bounty payments to encourage New England codfishery

1818, Convention of 1818 gives U.S. fishermen liberty to fish off Newfoundland and Labrador and to dry fish on those unsettled shores

1820, New Jersey permits individuals to store oysters on unoccupied sea bottom, thereby allowing private control of formerly common ground, followed by similar legislation in Rhode Island (1827), Maryland (1830), and Connecticut (1842)

1820-65, use of oyster dredges prohibited in Maryland for fear of overfishing

1830s, New England fishermen begin to fish regularly for cod and halibut on Georges Bank, east of Cape Cod

ca. 1835, commercial fishery for menhaden established in southern New England to produce industrial oil and fishmeal for fertilizer

ca. 1840, William Underwood's canning process to preserve food adopted for lobsters and oysters

Along the waterfront at Mystic Seaport, split and salted codfish are often displayed near the fishing schooner *L.A. Dunton*. For New England fishermen, codfish has been the most enduring resource of the sea. After European explorers discovered the wealth of cod in the North Atlantic, this fish, preserved with salt, became a prime commodity of trade and elevated Gloucester, Massachusetts, to one of the world's leading fishing ports. Mystic Seaport preserves the 1921 fishing schooner *L.A. Dunton*, one of the last of the thousands of vessels that fished under sail from New England, to represent the fisherman's way of life at sea. (Judy Beisler photo)

1800s. New England traders went all the way to the North Pacific to obtain sea otter pelts for trade with China. Others sailed in search of the remote rocks of the South Atlantic and North Pacific where seals gathered. Butchered for their skins, which were sold in China and Europe, several species of seal were driven to the edge of extinction by the remorseless sealers.

The hunt for whales also expanded greatly after 1820. Most northeastern ports entered the industry at least briefly, but through the 1800s it was centered in Nantucket and New Bedford, Massachusetts, and New London, Connecticut. By 1845, when 731 U.S. vessels and more than 20,000 men were engaged in whaling, the fleet was three times the size of all the other whaling fleets of the world combined. American whalers had entered the South Atlantic by the time of the American Revolution, and they first ventured into the Pacific in 1790. As maritime pioneers they hunted whales along the west coast of South America; across the Pacific in 1818; to the coast of Japan in 1819; to Hawai'i in 1820; through the Indian Ocean in the 1830s; to the Northwest Coast by 1835; into the eastern Arctic in the 1840s; to Baja California in 1845; and through the Bering Strait into the western Arctic Ocean after 1848.

"At the present day not one in two of the many thousand men before the mast employed in the American whale fishery, are Americans born," wrote Herman Melville in *Moby-Dick*, and even if he exaggerated slightly, he was correct that a whaleship's forecastle contained perhaps the most diverse society at sea. Young rural men seeking adventure at sea were joined by luckless immigrants and wandering sailors, African American mariners, and natives of the many islands visited by whaleships. "Islanders seem to make the best whalemen," Melville continued, and islanders from the Azores, Cape Verdes, Hawai'i, and the other Polynesian islands were recruited by visiting whalemen, but in the encounter the island cultures underwent great change.

The complex society of a whaleship might be further diversified by the presence of the captain's wife. More than 400 captains' wives are known to have accompanied their husbands on whaling voyages. Pioneers themselves, living an unconventional life, they saw far more of the world than their landbound sisters, even confined aboard ship. Some, like Sallie Smith, were bored by the isolation and lack of variety, while others were fascinated spectators of the voyage and whaling process. As her ship approached the Arctic Ocean on 12 July 1849, Mary Brewster of Stonington, Connecticut, gazed on the coasts of "Asia & America and I thought I was the first civilized female who had passed through the [Bering] straits," she recorded in her journal (now in Mystic Seaport's G.W. Blunt White Library).

Whalemen are known for their decorative art of scrimshaw—carving or engraving whale ivory, bone, or baleen—but their daily life was far from romantic. Whalemen spent much of their time scanning the sea to "raise" a whale. Whales were attacked with a whaleship's whaleboats, each of which carried an officer, a harpooner, and four seamen. When they reached the whale, the harpooner darted a harpoon into the whale, connecting it to the whaleboat by a long line, and then the men pulled the boat up to the exhausted whale so the officer could lance it to death. Often enough during this dangerous work, a whale lashed out with its tail flukes or jaws and smashed the whaleboat and injured or killed the crew. If they killed the whale, the crew towed it back to the whaleship, stripped off the layer of blubber, extracted the spermaceti from the sperm whale's head or the baleen from other whales' jaws, and rendered the blubber into oil in the tryworks on deck. For their labors, which might add up to three or more years on board before the voyage ended,

The *Charles W. Morgan*, now preserved at Mystic Seaport, was laid up in 1921, after 80 years and 37 whaling voyages.

1845, U.S. whaling fleet reaches largest size, with 731 active vessels

1846, first New England fishing schooner carries ice to preserve fresh halibut

1848, African American shipsmith Lewis Temple invents toggle harpoon, greatly increasing efficiency of whaling

Overfishing on Georges Bank seriously depletes halibut stocks in those waters

Captain Thomas Welcome Roys in the whaleship *Superior* passes through the Bering Strait into the Arctic Ocean, expanding the whale fishery north of the Arctic Circle

ca. 1848, canning of steamed oysters begins in Baltimore, increasing greatly after 1864

1851, Herman Melville publishes *Moby-Dick*

ca. 1854, Treaty of Medicine Creek secures Indian fishing rights in the Northwest

71

ca. 1855, Connecticut oystermen begin to practice aquaculture, buying or leasing underwater plots and taking young oysters from natural beds to grow in these artificial beds

1859, first successful oil well drilled at Titusville, Pennsylvania, introducing age of petroleum

1862, registered tonnage of U.S. deep-sea fishing vessels reaches highest point

1864, Hume brothers of Maine establish a salmon cannery in California, moving to the Columbia River in 1867, which initiates a large-scale salmon fishery from California to Alaska

ca. 1865, longline trawl, equipped with hundreds of hooks and set from dories, becomes primary method of catching bottom-dwelling fish

Maryland limits oyster dredging to sailing vessels

At about age 25, Captain Lorenzo Dow Baker (1815-94) of Groton, Connecticut, looking the part of a proud sailor with his earrings, posed in front of a whaling scene to depict his trade. Whaling offered opportunities for skilled young men willing to endure long isolation and occasional danger at sea. As an alternative to a life on the farm, Baker went to sea at about age 16 on board a whaleship from Stonington, Connecticut. At 18, on his third voyage, he was a harpooner, becoming first mate at 22 and captain at 24. As captain, he made five whaling voyages over 15 years. When the local whaling industry declined in the late 1850s, Baker took command of the clipper ship *Hound*, carrying cargo to San Francisco, and remained in merchant service until retiring. (Mystic Seaport, 36.5)

Sallie Smith did not enjoy life on a whaleship, but she made two voyages with her Captain husband. (Mystic Seaport, 41.29.1)

whalemen received a "lay," a small share of the profits of the voyage.

In *Moby-Dick* Herman Melville proclaimed: "But though the world scouts at us whale hunters, yet does it unwittingly pay us the profoundest homage; yea, an all-abounding adoration! For almost all the tapers, lamps, and candles that burn round the globe, burn, as before so many shrines, to our glory!" As Melville suggested, the oil rendered from the whale's insulating blubber was processed to produce lamp oil used in U.S. lighthouses as well as in house lamps across the nation. As factory production of textiles and other manufactured goods expanded, whale oil found new uses as a lubricant for machinery. Sperm whale oil was the finest lubricant, and the cleanest burning oil, and the waxy spermaceti still made the best candles. The other whale product of value (besides the ambergris occasionally recovered from sick sperm whales, which was used as a perfume base) was the baleen—called "whalebone" by whalemen—from the mouths of nontoothed whales. This flexible material was used in ways we would use plastic today, from stiffening women's corsets to making umbrella ribs and buggy whips.

The whaling industry began a long decline in the 1850s. The increasing length of voyages to find enough whales, better economic return in other industries, competition from other oil products (especially with the development of the petroleum industry after 1859) and losses to Confederate commerce raiders during the Civil War, reduced the size of the American whaling fleet.

Whaling Captain George Comer photographed these Inuits inside an igloo near Hudson Bay, ca. 1904. Whaling brought American mariners into contact with native peoples around the world. Soon after whaleships first called at Hawai'i and South Pacific Islands for supplies, they began to recruit native men for whaling. Later, whalers in the Arctic also employed native whalemen. The man in the checked shirt, called Harry by Comer and the whalemen, worked for Comer as a whaler in Hudson Bay for 20 years. Many island cultures changed dramatically after contact with Euro-American mariners. Captain Comer was among the few mariners who actively studied and appreciated the cultures with which they interacted. Comer photographed and even recorded the Inuits, and collected information and artifacts on their culture. (Mystic Seaport, 66.399.36)

1866, elimination of federal bounty to support codfishing vessels

ca. 1867, purse seine fishnet becomes primary method of catching surface-schooling fish, especially menhaden and mackerel

1868, Maryland establishes "Oyster Navy," the Maryland Marine Police, to preserve order between oyster tongers and oyster dredgers

1871, September, American whaling fleet in Arctic Ocean on north coast of Alaska trapped by ice, with the loss of 32 vessels; 1,200 whalemen, with a few captains' wives and children, are rescued

ca. 1874, first steam-powered fishing vessels built for coastal use in oyster and menhaden fisheries

1874, Maine begins to set open season for lobstering and minimum size for harvesting lobsters to conserve species

1878, canned "codfish balls" (cod and potato cakes) introduced for consumer convenience

1878, first salmon cannery in Alaska opens

1879, greatest annual loss of life in the New England fisheries, with 29 vessels and 249 fishermen lost at sea

1883, 25 January, dorymates Howard Blackburn and Thomas Walsh go astray in fog while fishing 100 miles off Newfoundland; Walsh dies but Blackburn rows to shore and survives, despite losing his fingers and toes to frostbite, setting the standard for the heroic endurance of Gloucester fishermen

1885, Maryland oystermen harvest a record 15,000,000 bushels of oysters

ca. 1888, beginning of commercial halibut fishing in Pacific Northwest

Congress suspends southern mackerel season for five years as experiment to conserve the species

1890, Maryland imposes minimum size for harvestable oysters

1896, Rudyard Kipling publishes *Captains Courageous,* a boy's coming of age aboard a fishing schooner

ca. 1898-1912, oyster production peaks in Northeast: nearly 25,000,000 pounds of oyster meat in New York, 15,000,000 in Connecticut, and 15,000,000 in Rhode Island

Although they were not saved for commercial purposes, sperm whale teeth have come to represent whaling because they were used in the whaleman's art of scrimshaw, carved or engraved in both decorative and useful forms as gifts and keepsakes during days of boredom at sea. During the 1878 voyage of the bark *Ohio,* Captain Fred Smith carved a variety of domestic items for his wife Sallie, who made the voyage with him. In her journal, she recorded teaching him to crochet with the scrimshaw needles he had made for her. (Mystic Seaport, 41.632.1-3, 41.632.2, 41.632.6)

In marketing its clam juice as a healthful product, ca. 1900, the Doxsee company celebrated the watermen whose hard work provided clams and other shellfish for American consumers. (Mystic Seaport, 81.98.14)

With the demand for baleen remaining high until after 1900, a small fleet continued to hunt whales, especially in the Arctic domains of the right and bowhead whales. In those waters, ice threatened the fleet even in summer. In 1871, a shift in the ice pack trapped and destroyed 32 American whaleships. The industry continued to decline until the last traditional American whaling voyage ended in 1928. A few U.S. companies engaged in the far more destructive form of whaling with cannon and factory ships, which produced oil, meat, and meal, until the U.S. proposed to the International Whaling Commission a moratorium on whaling in 1972.

Oils were also rendered from sea elephants of the south Indian Ocean, and extracted from cod livers, but another major source of oil was the menhaden. We think of fish as food, but few people would eat the oily, bony menhaden by choice, even when it was packed like sardines. When the fish was boiled and pressed however, valuable oil could be extracted for use as a preservative, and for paint, tanning, and other manufactured products. The leftover fishmeal, when dried, produced a valuable fertilizer. When these processes were developed around 1830, a fishery grew, eventually all along the East Coast and along the Gulf Coast 100 years later. To catch the large schools of menhaden that swam up the East Coast, fishermen developed the purse seine, a long wall of netting with a drawstring on the bottom, which was set in a circle around a school and then pursed up to capture the fish in a net bag. In the 1870s the fishery was the first to adopt steam-powered vessels to deliver the fish to the processing plants. Although it is largerly unseen by us today, the menhaden fishery is America's largest in terms of quantity of fish caught.

When it came to fish for food, American fishing methods changed little for 300 years. Like whaling, fishing voyages were usually "adventures," with the crew receiving a share of the profits (either divided evenly or according to their individual catch) rather than a wage. Because it was an essential industry which could train sailors for naval service, New England's codfishing industry was subsidized with a federal bounty between 1793 and 1866.

Then, between 1830 and 1930, almost everything about the ways Americans caught fish changed dramatically. Part of this was caused by the shift of fish from a commodity for overseas trade to a product for domestic consumption. The expanding nation required an abundance of protein, and salted cod, which was easy to ship and to store, became an important commodity in the South and in the West. At the same time, the growth of cities with railroad and steamboat connections to the coast increased the demand for fresh fish.

This demand led to the use of vessels with water-filled holds to keep fish alive, and then to experiments in the 1840s in carrying ice to sea to preserve freshly caught halibut. The success of these experiments encouraged year-round fishing on the offshore banks, but the dangers of winter fishing on the cold and stormy banks, often in vessels more suited to summer sailing, made fishing an increasingly dangerous occupation. By the 1880s larger, safer fishing schooners were being designed, and after 1900 the type was perfected with vessels like Mystic Seaport's *L.A. Dunton*.

In the hunt for bottom-dwelling fish, which the fishermen tracked with experience and intuition and caught with a great deal of exertion using handlines from the deck of their vessel, the shift to more efficient methods began around 1850. Both immigrant and Yankee fishermen began to use

1905, Bay State Fishing Company of Boston introduces otter trawl net fishing in New England offshore waters

ca. 1910, beginning of California tuna fishing and canned tuna

ca. 1915, with increased use of otter trawl fishnet, various species of flounder become common in the marketplace for the first time

To attract consumers, fish canners created appealing names and bold labels for their products. However similar the fish inside might be, the labels created an exclusive identity. Early efforts to can Columbia River sockeye and silver salmon first found a receptive market among working-men in Great Britain. As American consumers acquired a taste for canned salmon, the industry expanded to include the chum salmon of Washington's Puget Sound, and the far larger red salmon resources of coastal Alaska. Much of the annual pack of Alaska salmon was controlled by the Alaska Packers Association of San Francisco, which operated most of the seasonal canneries, shipping fishermen and cannery workers north in the spring and shipping the pack south for distribution around the country at the end of the season. (Mystic Seaport, 99.38.3)

1914, first fishing schooner equipped with diesel engine

1921, boneless filet of fish developed for consumer convenience

ca. 1922, following postwar recession, number of wooden-hulled, powered "draggers" expands to exceed number of sail-powered schooners in New England

1925, Clarence Birdseye patents quick-freezing method of preserving food, which is applied to boneless fish filet for consumer convenience

ca. 1925, shrimp fishermen in Gulf of Mexico adopt use of otter trawl and engine-powered boats, greatly increasing shrimp harvest

Oyster fishery in Northeast states enters decline, partly due to coastal pollution and public concern over disease

ca. 1927, quantity of New England groundfish caught by net first exceeds quantity caught by hook and line

1928, last traditional American whaling voyage ends at San Francisco

1932, first "crash" of haddock stocks on Georges Bank suggests the possibility of overfishing

1933, start of construction on Bonneville Dam (completed 1937) and Grand Coulee Dam (completed 1941) to produce hydroelectric power on Columbia River, which produce vast amounts of electric power and water for irrigation, but create major impediments to salmon migration

the European trawl line, which was anchored along the bottom, with several hundred hooks attached at intervals. Using a trawl line, two fishermen could catch three times as many fish as they could with handlines. However, this method required that they leave their vessel to set their lines. Their fishing schooners now became mother ships to fleets of dories, flat-bottom fishing boats originally used for fishing off the beach. Simply yet strongly built, stable when loaded, and able to be stacked on deck like spoons, dories proved to be surprisingly seaworthy when used on the open sea as much as 100 miles offshore. This method predominated from the Civil War to nearly 1930. Rudyard Kipling's *Captains Courageous* presents a vivid picture of life in dory fishing schooners.

European fishermen shifted to nets in the 1800s, and New England fishermen began to experiment with netting bottom-dwelling fish before 1895. Ten years later, a British-style steam vessel began to fish out of Boston, dragging a large net "otter trawl" across the bottom, and proved that "dragging" was twice as productive as fishing with hook and line. After the internal combustion engine was perfected for use at sea through the 1920s, powered draggers drove sailing dory schooners from the sea. With some refinements in vessel design and the shift to handling the nets at the stern, this method has predominated ever since.

On the surface, fishermen designed large nets to increase their catches. Mackerel fishermen adopted the purse seine to capture this flavorful schooling fish, which remained extremely popular among Americans through the 1930s. Alongshore, early fishermen had used simple nets or Native American brush weirs to intercept fish. In the Northeast, and later in the Great Lakes, they built large net structures called traps or pounds to direct fish into a central compartment. The gill net, which snared fish as they swam through, was another passive method of fishing, which trapped fish even when fishermen went about other business. Traps and gill nets became especially productive in the salmon fisheries of the Columbia River, Puget Sound, and Alaska, which led all U.S. fisheries in the quantity of fish caught by 1900.

Alongshore, some of the seasonal fisheries supported farmer-fishermen, who worked the local fishing season and methods into their agricultural cycle. The menhaden fishery first used local labor during its six-month season. As the fishery expanded into the South in the 1870s however, African Americans increasingly became the labor force for the menhaden industry.

76

Milton J. Burns's dramatic painting of a fishing schooner picking up a dory during a gale suggests the new level of risk introduced by dory fishing. While vessel designs had become safer and better able to weather such conditions by the 1890s, dory fishermen were exposed year-round to unpredictable weather far from shore. They continued to work for a share of the profits, but these men were increasingly immigrant laborers, pursuing their skills in dangerous conditions to succeed in the land of opportunity. Consumers had little idea of the hazards fishermen endured to put fish on the table. (Mystic Seaport, 75.293)

1940, canned tuna surpasses canned salmon in quantity and popularity

1946, menhaden fishery established in Gulf of Mexico with factories in Alabama, Mississippi, Louisiana, and Texas

1947, first offshore oil well drilled in Gulf of Mexico

ca. 1950, frozen fried "fish sticks" introduced for convenience of fish preparation

ca. 1953, beginning of king crab fishery in stormy winter seas of Gulf of Alaska and Bering Sea

1957, Dalles Dam on the Columbia River submerges Celilo Falls, a traditional Native-American fishing site, symbolizing the significance of hydroelectric power over environmental or cultural considerations during much of the 1900s

1960, Soviet factory trawlers first arrive on Georges Bank, beginning rapid increase of overharvesting of groundfish on Northwest Atlantic banks

1965, first catfish farm established in Humphreys County, Mississippi

1969, Connecticut first permits powered dredge boats to harvest oysters on natural beds as local fishery begins to revive

1972, with increase of European "distant water" trawlers, U.S. fishermen take only 10 percent of groundfish caught on Georges Bank

International Whaling Commission proposes ban on all whaling

Most fisheries, however, employed full-time fishermen, an increasing number of whom were the maritime equivalent of migrant laborers. By the late 1800s safer, more lucrative jobs ashore in New England or farther west were attracting the young men who might have gone fishing. In their place, young men from maritime Canada, Ireland, Scandinavia, and the Portuguese islands of the Azores and Cape Verdes came to work in the New England fleet, where they could earn more money and live better than at home. Some of these men drifted south to work in the expanding fisheries of the Gulf of Mexico in winter, while Scandinavian fishermen established themselves in the net fisheries of the Great Lakes and especially the netting of salmon in the Pacific Northwest. By 1900, Italian fishermen were active in Massachusetts, as well as in California where they began the commercial tuna fishery about 1910.

When fish processing became a more diversified industry, labor expanded there as well. As in other handwork industries such as textiles, women found employment before 1850. Before the Civil War, women had begun shucking oysters in the shops around New Haven, Connecticut, as they did later in the oyster packing houses of Baltimore and the oyster and shrimp plants of the Gulf Coast around New Orleans and Biloxi. Women also

Waiting for the mackerel to rise, these fishermen rest on their oars in antici-
pation of a mad dash to surround a school of fish with their purse seine.
Between 1830 and 1930 the U.S. fishing industry was revolutionized by the
development of purse seines to enclose schools of surface fish, of gill nets and
fish traps to snare individual fish, and of otter trawl nets to drag up bottom
fish in quantities never before possible. Milton J. Burns painted this view ca.
1880. (Mystic Seaport, 75.291; Mary Anne Stets photo)

1974, Judge George Boldt rules that U.S. treaties with Indians along the Columbia River reserve half the salmon harvest for those tribes, thus limiting commercial salmon fishing in the Columbia and encouraging tribal participation in management of Columbia River salmon resources

1977, by terms of 1976 Magnuson Act, U.S. declares 200-mile coastal exclusion zones, restricting foreign fishing vessels from free access to fishing banks, and establishes regional councils to manage fisheries

1980s, U.S. offshore fishing fleet expands, and most regional councils adopt policy of "maximum sustainable yield," resulting in catches exceeding renewable stocks of various species, including king crab in the Northwest and cod, haddock, and summer flounder off New England

Following lead of Asian nations, U.S. factory trawlers begin to catch Alaska pollock for use as frozen white fish or surimi, helping make this the principal food fish caught by quantity

1982, International Whaling Commission issues ban on commercial whaling

worked in the early lobster and sardine canneries of Maine; in the sardine canneries at Monterey, California; in the firms that processed and packed boneless salt cod in various forms around Gloucester, Massachusetts; and in the expanding salmon canning industry of the Pacific Northwest.

Eastern European workers who had emigrated to Baltimore found seasonal work canning oysters and vegetables in Maryland, heading to the Gulf ports to can oysters and shrimp in winter. On the West Coast, Chinese salmon butchers were highly regarded for their skill and endurance in the salmon canneries, although racist immigration laws increasingly limited their ability to enter the U.S. By 1910 mechanized processing had taken their place as the salmon industry became the leader among U.S. fisheries.

As fishermen delivered increasing quantities and varieties of fish, processors found new ways of making it convenient for consumers. Canning was the leading method for salmon, tuna, sardines, oysters, and shrimp, and boxes of boneless salt cod were useful for immigrants and for those living far from the sea. In the 1920s, Massachusetts processors introduced the boneless filet of fish, and Clarence Birdseye developed a method for quick-freezing fish. As a result, since 1930 the boneless frozen filet of white

78

fish has become most popular, while there is little demand for strong-tasting, seasonal fish like mackerel.

The development of the internal combustion engine led to a great increase in the demand for petroleum. Oil reserves were tapped to the edge of the sea in California and Texas, and then in 1947 a floating rig ventured into the Gulf of Mexico to drill in shallow water. With the success of this experiment, production rigs sprouted alongshore. The Gulf rigs stood among the fishing grounds for shrimp and menhaden, but for the most part did not harm fish stocks through spillage. By the 1990s computerized operations, flexible piping, and floating production rigs have pushed petroleum and natural gas recovery into thousands of feet of water. The new 1,900-foot Baldpate compliant tower, standing in 1,650 feet of water, is the world's tallest free-standing structure. Nevertheless, the possibility of catastrophic damage to an oil well in exposed waters has so far kept the petroleum industry from invading some of the richest fishing grounds, especially Georges Bank.

Since 1950, our relentless search and consumption of wild seafood has brought species after species to the edge of extinction. Radar, sonar, and electronic navigational methods developed for naval use during and after World War II have removed much of the guesswork from finding fish in the sea. Powerful, economical engines, and freezing

1984, because of U.S. and Canadian claims under 200-mile exclusion zone provisions, World Court partitions Georges Bank, awarding eastern tip to Canadian control

1986, Congress requires Federal Energy Regulatory Commission to consider environmental protection when licensing hydroelectric projects

1994, Fishing grounds on Georges Bank off Massachusetts closed to fishing to allow recovery of fish stocks

1994-95, Congress authorizes funds to buy fishing vessels, providing compensation for fishermen willing to give up fishing

1998, U.S. and Canada go to court over status of Northwest Coast salmon that spawn in Canadian rivers but are caught by U.S. fishermen on the high seas

1999, tallest manmade structure in the world, a 1,900-foot-tall oil rig, placed in 1,650 feet of water on Baldpate Bank in the Gulf of Mexico

In Washington State, Makah whalers kill one gray whale in revival of tribal whaling traditions

In a notable reversal of previous policy, federal government requires breaching of 162-year-old dam on the Kennebec River at Augusta, Maine, for environmental reasons, allowing salmon 17 miles further upstream

At an oyster house in Baltimore, Maryland, around 1900, women shuck tons of oysters to be canned. Baltimore pioneered oyster canning in the 1840s, making this delectable seafood available all over the country. The handwork required for processing or canning shellfish—oysters, scallops, lobsters, crabs, and shrimp—as well as salmon and sardines, provided employment opportunities for women and a variety of immigrant and minority groups in many coastal communities. (Mystic Seaport, 91.5.3)

FOR HEALTH, VARIETY and NOURISHMENT SERVE FISH and SEA FOOD EACH DAY

By the 1920s, when fresh or frozen seafood could be shipped almost anywhere in the U.S., it had begun to be promoted for its healthful effects. The U.S. Fisheries Association was one of a number of national organizations that encouraged consumption of the nation's increasing catch of fish and shellfish. Seafood is still considered health food, although pollution and overharvesting have changed our perceptions of this resource of the sea. (Mystic Seaport, 97.23.1, Judy Beisler photo)

As overfishing has depleted many species of ocean fish, aquaculture—"fish farming"—has been seen as a possible alternative to capture of "wild" fish. Though not free of environmental concerns, U.S. aquaculture has been very successful with catfish. Hundreds of millions of pounds of catfish are harvested annually from artificial ponds on catfish farms across the former "cotton belt" from Alabama to Arkansas. (Courtesy Catfish Institute; Lou Manna photo)

plants on board have allowed vessels to go farther in search of fish and deliver them in good condition. And the ability to ship fresh fish around the world has expanded the demand for the most popular species. The European "distant water trawlers" that first crossed the North Atlantic around 1960 increased the pressure on American fishermen. The Magnuson Act of 1976 sought to protect the economic interests of U.S. fishermen by excluding foreign-flag vessels from grounds within 200 miles of the U.S. coast and turning over management of protected species to regional councils composed of interested individuals. Most regional councils adopted a policy of "maximum sustainable yield," resulting in large catches that seriously depleted various species, including king crab in the Northwest and cod, haddock, scallops, and summer flounder off New England.

The last 20 years of the 1900s demonstrated challenges of gathering the living resources of the sea. Skilled men and women, some of whom still represent recent immigrant groups, continue to find satisfaction in taking their living from the sea, using better, more precise equipment than ever before. Inshore, under jurisdiction of individual states, there have been successes in managing the harvest of shellfish, such as lobsters in Maine, and in restoring populations of others, such as oysters in Long Island Sound. And, despite the expense and the risks of disease in a captive population, aquaculture has proven to be an alternative for some kinds of "wild" fish, notably catfish "farming" in manmade pools across part of the former "cotton belt" of the deep South, shrimp and tilapia raising, and Atlantic salmon "farming" in ocean pens in Maine. But the many forms of pollution from our coastal living have severely damaged many prime fishing areas, such as Chesapeake Bay, and competing uses, such as the hydroelectric and irrigation projects along the Columbia River, have altered the environment in ways that will require many years to restore.

Offshore, the concept of the sea as a vast commons open to all has come into question. By the 1990s the federal government had stepped in to regulate fishing with quotas on endangered species, with closure of overworked fishing grounds, notably Georges Bank, and with an initial reduction in the fishing fleet through vessel purchase. At the same time, large factory trawlers catch record quantities of Alaska pollock, a previously underused fish, that go into the surimi (textured fish protein) and frozen fish patties that have become common convenience foods.

How do we balance our demand for the cheap, healthful protein of seafood and the fisherman's desire to make a rewarding living at sea with our ability to catch more fish than can be reproduced naturally? Must fishermen, who are now the last commercial hunters and trappers, become farmers of the sea in the future to provide seafood? How do we balance our demand for hydroelectric power, timber, and cheap food grown on irrigated land with the need to keep rivers unobstructed and clean to support natural populations of salmon and other fish? How do we ensure that the habitat for marine life is not degraded as our activities increase in the coastal zone and we tap the sea bottom for petroleum and gas? These are the challenges of the twenty-first century as we attempt to manage our limited resources in a way that does not destroy them, or us.

In Alaska, on the frontier of American fishing, Theresa Peterson fishes offshore for halibut, using a modern version of the trawl line with its many baited hooks. Alaska leads the nation in the value of food-fish caught, and those who fish there combine tradition and innovation to survive some of the harshest conditions faced by the American fishing fleet. (Courtesy Theresa Peterson)

Despite the uncertainties of fishing today, thousands of Americans are devoted to the way of life. As a fisherman's son, John Rita of Stonington, Connecticut, realized at an early age that he wanted to follow his father and other Portuguese fishermen of Stonington. "I just loved being on the water. . . . being free, doing what you like to do," Rita said. He has commanded the 48-foot dragger *Seafarer* since 1986, fishing alongshore for flounder and squid. (Mary Anne Stets photo)

81

Part Seven
FINDING INSPIRATION

The sea has shaped America's culture just as it has shaped our coastline. Maritime images have filled our lives for so long that many of us take them for granted. Our fine and decorative arts, our music and literature—even our language itself—all reflect the influence of the sea and seafaring on our lives.

Just as the sea's awesome grandeur has nourished our artists, writers, musicians, and dreamers, its power has inspired feats of bravery and heroism that have become part of our national mythology. When Americans really want to test themselves, they still go to sea.

Sailors go to sea to work. But even those who are isolated by the sea, who know the awesome power of water, and whose hours are shaped by the demands of operating a vessel can find creative expression there. The "arts of the sailor," the functional and decorative knotwork practiced on board, or the decorative embroidery of naval uniforms, were the simplest ways in which the sea influenced the creativity of mariners. Whalemen might pass the time on their long voyages by carving or engraving whale ivory and bone into fanciful or practical items.

As ocean pioneers, sailors were the first to adopt the Polynesian artform of tattooing to adorn their bodies with images of luck, religious faith, patriotism, or sentimental family associations. Well into the 1800s, sailors often adorned themselves with earrings in a superstitious effort to enhance their eyesight. Sailors also created rituals symbolic of their life apart from the land, such as the "crossing the line" ceremony, when novice sailors were initiated by an "old salt" dressed as the sea god Neptune while their ship crossed the equator.

The language of the sea was also specific to the work and conditions of the sea, often combining words old and new from different languages in a sort of "creole" amalgam of the ocean world. Some of the sailor's jargon has been adapted into our everyday language of the land. Terms common to us, such as scuttlebut, leeway, or deep six, were once the folk language of sailors.

Illustration on page 82: An icon of the sea in gold and silver, the Palladium Cup with its representation of the sea god Neptune was presented to the New Haven, Connecticut, Yacht Club in the 1880s as an award for sailboat races. (Mystic Seaport, 57.291)

Shadowbox models were one form of sailor's folk art. This one of a full-rigged American ship was made by Arthur Henderson in 1920. (Mystic Seaport, 53.3972)

Some sailors took up modeling, building small representations of their vessels in their spare time. As crude as these might be, pieced together with few tools from scraps found on board ship, the rigging of sailor-made models was usually extremely accurate because sailors were most familiar with that part of their vessels. One form of model was the shadowbox, like a three-dimensional painting with a half-model and scene set in a shallow frame. The most elaborate sailors' models were produced by captive seamen in British prisons during the Napoleonic Wars and War of 1812. These highly detailed bone models of warships, some of which were built by American sailors, display a precise creativity.

Throughout American history, the sea has figured prominently in the fine arts of painting, poetry, and literature. Ship portraits celebrate the vehicles of the sea. The variety of surviving ship portraits, painted in Liverpool by Samuel Walters, in Marseilles by members of the Roux family, in Hong Kong by Lai Sung, and by many other artists at ports in between, show the reach of American ships in the 1800s. American marine artists like James Bard or Antonio Jacobsen, and less-skilled pier-head painters like William P. Stubbs, also recorded the nation's coastal and ocean vessels. As skilled as many of these artists were at rendering ships naturally, their works are more valued today for their historic value than as emotional expressions of the sea.

Many other artists of the 1800s used the sea as the subject or backdrop for their explorations of the world. Building on Dutch, English, and French traditions of maritime art in the 1600s and 1700s, American artists expressed a romantic idealism through natural scenes. Artists such as Thomas Birch and Fitz Hugh Lane specialized in port scenes, though Lane's luminous views of the Maine coast are similar to the grand perspectives of the "Hudson River School" of artists such as Thomas Cole, Frederic Edwin Church, and the even more luminous work of John Frederick Kensett, Martin Johnson Heade, or William Bradford. James Buttersworth combined the play of light on clouds and the sea with dramatic perspectives of ships and their tiny sailors awash in a boisterous ocean. In these works, humans are often dwarfed by the sea, bold riverscapes, and flaming or threatening skies. During the same years, George Caleb Bingham romanticized the life of the free-spirited Mississippi River boatmen, while other artists celebrated the advance of steamboat technology to master the rivers.

A later generation of artists placed humans more prominently in relation to the sea. Winslow Homer turned to the sea and inland waters in the 1870s, creating hopeful images such as *Breezing Up*, fluid watercolors of mountain fishing and Florida workboats, as well as more intimidating views of the sea's menacing power in his later work. Thomas Eakins turned an incisive eye to boating near Philadelphia, composing paintings that are both character studies and accurate depictions of river life.

At the same time, illustrators such as Milton J. Burns rendered dramatic maritime images to illustrate the

1835-1907, Currier and Ives, America's most prolific lithographic firm, publishes over 350 maritime scenes among their 4,000 popular images

ca. 1835-65, Fitz Hugh Lane paints luminous scenes around Gloucester, Massachusetts, Boston, and Maine

1839-44, Herman Melville spends time at sea aboard a merchant ship, a whaleship, and a naval vessel

1851, Herman Melville publishes *Moby-Dick*

ca. 1859, Samuel Clemens spends three years training to become a Mississippi River pilot, later adopting Mark Twain (two fathoms, or 12 feet of depth to the river pilot) as his literary name

1870s-90s, art colonies established in various coastal locations, including Provincetown and Cape Ann, Massachusetts, Old Lyme and Cos Cob, Connecticut, and Easthampton, Long Island, New York, frequented by American realist and impressionist artists such as Winslow Homer, Henry Ward Ranger, Childe Hassam, Edward and Thomas Moran, and J.H. Twachtman

1873-1919, after emigrating from Denmark, Antonio Jacobsen becomes ship portrait painter in the port of New York, completing 2,600 paintings during his 45-year career

ca. 1873-1909, Winslow Homer paints coastal and river fishing scenes in oil and watercolor, including *Breezing Up* (1876)

ca. 1874-87, Thomas Eakins paints boating scenes on the Delaware and Schuylkill Rivers

A sailor on board the schooner *Herbert L. Rawding* in 1924 shows off his models. (Courtesy John Van Horn)

85

Tattooing became a popular art form for sailors, especially after Pacific voyagers encountered it in cultures around the Pacific in the late 1700s. As part of the culture of the sea, sailors adorned themselves with a variety of designs, from simple symbols to intricate figures like this, offered by Providence, Rhode Island, tattoo artist C.H. Fellowes, ca. 1900. (Mystic Seaport, 83.52.3; Jennifer M. Stich photo)

1874, Mark Twain (Samuel Clemens) publishes *Life on the Mississippi*

1876, Mark Twain publishes *Adventures of Tom Sawyer*

1877, 28 May, Captain and Mrs. Thomas Crapo sail across the Atlantic from New Bedford to Penzance in a 20-foot sailboat

1884, Mark Twain publishes *Adventures of Huckleberry Finn*

1895, 24 April to 28 June 1898, Captain Joshua Slocum sails alone around the world

1896, 6 June to 7 August, George Harbo and Frank Samuelson row across the Atlantic, from New York to Le Havre

1896-97, Rudyard Kipling publishes *Captains Courageous*

popular magazines of the day. Since 1900 artists as varied as Maurice Prendergast, Edward Hopper, Jackson Pollock, and Andrew and James Wyeth have placed settings, patterns, or colors from the sea in their work.

Like the romantic artists, poets have sought greater meaning in the sea. Ralph Waldo Emerson presented the sea as a positive force in his "Sea-Shore."

> *. . .Sea full of foods, the nourisher of all kinds,*
> *Purger of earth, and medicine of men;*
> *Creating a sweet climate by my breath,*
> *Washing out harms and griefs from memory,*
> *And, in my mathematic ebb and flow,*
> *Giving a hint of that which changes not.*

Walt Whitman took verse offshore into the unsettling world of the ship in his poem, "In Cabin'd Ships at Sea."

> *. . . The sky o'erarches here, we feel the undulating deck*
> *   beneath our feet,*
> *We feel the long pulsation, ebb and flow of endless motion,*
> *The tones of unseen mystery, the vague and vast*
> *   suggestions of the briny world, the liquid flowing*
> *   syllables. . .*

Langston Hughes evoked the essential relationship in "The Negro Speaks of Rivers."

> *I've known rivers:*
> *I've known rivers ancient as the world and older than the*
> *   flow of human blood in human veins.*
>
> *My soul has grown deep like the rivers . . .*

As Whitman suggested in "Crossing Brooklyn Ferry," our attraction to the sea is timeless.

> *. . . Just as you feel when you look on the river and sky, so I felt,*
> *Just as any of you is one of a living crowd, I was one of a*
> *   crowd,*
> *Just as you are refresh'd by the gladness of the river and the*
> *   bright flow, I was refresh'd,*
> *Just as you stand and lean on the rail, yet hurry with the*
> *   swift current, I stood yet was hurried, . . .*

Much of America's classic literature is linked to the sea. James Fenimore Cooper drew on his own experience when writing the earliest American sea novels, *The Pilot*, *The Red Rover*, and *The Water-Witch* (1824-30). Herman

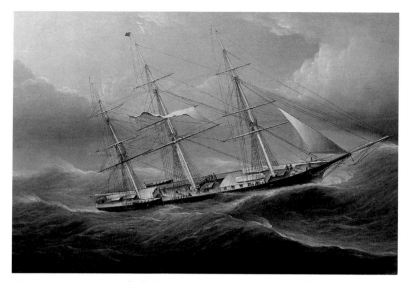

Artists continue to find inspiration in the power of the sea. James Buttersworth painted this image of a clipper ship fighting a gale, ca. 1855. (Mystic Seaport, 49.3176)

Melville's maritime experience helped him compose several sea novels, including the dense book that is often considered the greatest work of American fiction, *Moby-Dick*. Some of the best of Mark Twain's fiction is propelled by the Mississippi River, where he learned the pilot's art before the Civil War. In their works, these authors created authentic American voices that reflected our national ties to the maritime world.

Although Jack London wrote stories of Pacific fishermen and sealers, and Eugene O'Neill spoke for the dehumanized crews of ocean steamships in several of his plays, the sea fiction of the 1900s has emphasized naval themes, from Herman Wouk's *Caine Mutiny* to Tom Clancy's *Hunt for Red October*. But even if our contemporary novelists have less sea experience to share, it is no less true that "The voice of the sea is seductive; never ceasing, whispering, clamoring, murmuring, inviting the soul to wander for a spell in abysses of solitude; to lose itself in mazes of inward contemplation," as Kate Chopin wrote in *The Awakening* (1899).

Images of the sea, ships, and sailors have long been a part of our popular vocabulary, from clothing to music. For more than 150 years, songs and their accompanying sheet music have featured the sea in songs of parting, loss, and reunion. The songs of sailors and fishermen—the working chanteys and the off-duty fo'c'sle songs—also came ashore, preserved as folk music, especially as the way of life that created them came to an end in the 1900s. By the 1900s the sea also represented recreation in popular

1898, the short story, "The Open Boat" published by Stephen Crane

1902-2000, N.C. Wyeth begins career of distinctively realistic painting often illustrating sea and coastal themes, which also appear in the works of his son Andrew Wyeth, who began painting in the 1930s, and his grandson James Wyeth, who began working in the 1960s

1904, Jack London publishes *The Sea Wolf*

1906, one of the year's hit songs is "Anchors Aweigh"

1907, one of the year's hit songs is "Bell Bottom Trousers"

"The Steerage" photograph by Alfred Stieglitz

1911, Metropolitan Museum of Art opens major Winslow Homer exhibition

1911-16, George Bellows paints Maine maritime scenes in the socially conscious style of the "Ashcan School"

1912, RMS *Titanic* sinks

Motorboat *Detroit* makes first motorboat crossing of the Atlantic

1922, Eugene O'Neill's play, *The Hairy Ape*, dramatizes the dehumanization of the men who stoked the boilers of steamships

1923, African American poet Langston Hughes goes to sea aboard a merchant ship

1926, Bronx-born Gertrude Ederle swims the English Channel in 14 hours 31 minutes, breaking the existing record by 2 hours

1926, *Show Boat* written by Edna Ferber; becomes a hit Broadway musical by Oscar Hammerstein II and Jerome Kern in 1927, and a hit movie in 1936

1928, Disney produces the first animated feature with sound, *Steamboat Willie*, starring a mouse called Mickey

1929, cartoon character Popeye the Sailor is created; appears as an animated series in 1933

1935-37, training ship *Joseph Conrad* circumnavigates the globe with young mariners

1937, film version of *Captains Courageous* stars Spencer Tracy, directed by Victor Fleming

1938-68, Irving and Electa Johnson operate vessels named *Yankee* to take young Americans on voyages of discovery at sea

1947, Jackson Pollock's abstract painting, *Full Fathom Five*, breaks bonds of representational maritime painting

1952, Pulitzer prize for literature awarded to Herman Wouk for *The Caine Mutiny*

1953, Pulitzer prize for literature awarded to Ernest Hemingway for *The Old Man and the Sea*

1954, three notable maritime films released, including *The Caine Mutiny*, starring Humphrey Bogart, directed by Edward Dmytryck; *On The Waterfront*, starring Marlon Brando, directed by Elia Kazan; and *20,000 Leagues Under the Sea*, starring Kirk Douglas, directed by Richard Fleischer

1955, film *Mr. Roberts* stars Henry Fonda, directed by John Ford

Several generations of Americans were unconsciously linked to the sea through the popularity of the "sailor suit" as children's clothing. Thomas Chappell of New London, Connecticut, wears an especially detailed sailor suit in this formal portrait by Everett A. Scholfield, ca. 1891. (Mystic Seaport, 77.92.525)

music, a trend reflected in much sheet music of the 1910s and 1920s, and more recently epitomized by the surfing tunes of the Beach Boys in the 1960s.

With the development of engraving, and particularly after the perfection of lithography around 1800, popular images could be mass-produced. William J. Bennett produced a series of highly detailed American port views in the 1830s, and other accomplished marine artists produced prints, but far more common were the lithographs published by Nathaniel Currier and Currier & Ives between 1835 and 1907. Their images of clipper ships and other maritime scenes in the 1850s introduced many Americans to the maritime world that served them.

Before the Civil War, images of ships and sailors

88

represented economic prosperity. In that time, when private banks issued their own currency, images of notable ships like the transatlantic steamships of the Collins Line, or of regional types like a western-rivers steamboat, frequently appeared on banknotes, representing the maritime underpinnings of the national economy.

After the Civil War, as manufacturers sought images of national significance to identify their products, many consumer goods, from soap to tobacco, were represented by images of sailors or ships. The growth of the U.S. Navy, and especially its victory in the Spanish-American War, gave advertisers plenty of popular images with which to associate their products.

American filmmakers have often taken their inspiration from the sea. Their movies cover a broad range, from tales of maritime life, including *Down to the Sea in Ships* (1922) (which included Mystic Seaport's *Charles W. Morgan*) and *Captains Courageous* (1937), to the World War II naval films *The Fighting Sullivans* (1942), *Destroyer* (1943), *They Were Expendable* (1945), and *Victory at Sea*, to adventure films such as *Jaws* (1975), *Titanic* (1998), and *The Perfect Storm* (2000), to amusement films such as *Bikini Beach* (1964) and *The Endless Summer* (1966), to films of social conscience, from *On the Waterfront* (1954) to *Amistad* (1998). Through these images of the sea, this popular and influential medium has helped shape Americans' impressions of the sea and life around it.

Another form of inspiration is the challenge to excel. We are not creatures of the sea, and only by our wits and our technology can we survive there. Even the shortest passage, or the most relaxed swim off the beach, tests our skill.

As a setting for romance or adventure, the sea and shore continue to inspire filmmakers. (Mystic Seaport, 96.108.8)

As symbols of national prosperity, nautical themes were used throughout the nation in the 1800s. The five dollar note issued by the City of Omaha, Nebraska, in 1857 included a vignette of sailors watching the approach of a Collins Line steamship. (Mystic Seaport, 96.161.1)

Mrs. Lucien Loeser spent four days on the shattered steamship *San Francisco*. Describing their ordeal, her sister wrote: "It was useless to think of touching a life preserver as we did not wish to prolong our misery. We would remain on the wreck as long as she held together." Ambrotype, ca. 1857. (Mystic Seaport, 49.3198)

1964, New York's Operation Sail, the first international gathering of "tall ships" in the U.S.

1975, film *Jaws*, directed by Steven Spielberg

1989, sailboat *Thursday's Child* sails from New York to San Francisco in 80 days 20 hours, breaking the record set by the clipper ship *Flying Cloud* in 1854

1993, trimaran *Great American II* sails from San Francisco to Boston in 69 days 20 hours, breaking the record set by the clipper ship *Northern Light* in 1853

1994, Pulitzer prize for fiction awarded to E. Annie Proulx for *The Shipping News*

1999, Tori Murden rows across the Atlantic, the first woman to do so

When the sea was solely a place of work, sailors (and passengers) faced this fact daily. Heroic rescues of people in peril on the sea were the greatest tests of skill and endurance. On the open sea, sailors were normally ready to risk their lives to rescue strangers from another ship, knowing they might require similar assistance some day. Alongshore, a number of local rescue organizations on dangerous coasts were superseded by the U.S. Life-Saving Service in the 1870s, which became part of the U.S. Coast Guard in 1915. Like the surfmen of 1900, Coast Guard boat handlers of 2000 train to master the worst sea conditions for the sake of saving human lives.

By the mid 1800s some Americans began to challenge themselves at sea. In 1866, the first transatlantic yacht race tested recreational vessels and sailors (most of them professional crews) against the North Atlantic in winter. Eleven years later, Thomas Crapo, a whaling captain from New Bedford, Massachusetts, sailed across the Atlantic in a small boat, accompanied by his wife. In 1896, George Harbo and Frank Samuelson of New Jersey successfully rowed a boat across the Atlantic. Their passage came in the middle of what is still considered a maritime milestone: Captain Joshua Slocum's solo voyage around the world. This three-year trip, described by Slocum in his popular book, *Sailing Alone Around the World*, has inspired many Americans since its publication in 1900.

Shipwreck called forth heroic rescue efforts. On Christmas 1853 the large new American steamship *San Francisco* foundered in a northeast gale on her way to the Pacific with more than 600 soldiers, passengers, and crew on board. In the busy North Atlantic, the American ship *Antarctic* and bark *Kilby*, and the British ship *Three Bells* came upon the wreck and stood by until the weather permitted them to rescue the passengers. Finally, after two weeks on the shattered vessel, the last of the 506 survivors were taken off. For their selfless heroism a number of crew members were awarded medals, and Nathaniel Currier commemorated the event with this dramatic lithograph. (Mystic Seaport, 49.3198)

These early forms of extreme experience at sea were undertaken by mariners. With the increase in recreation after 1870, ordinary Americans also sought the challenges of the sea. Inshore, the canoe craze of the 1870s and 1880s inspired determined paddlers to make long-distance trips along the Atlantic coast, down the Mississippi River, or across open waters under sail. The marine engine offered new challenges. The river crossing of the motorboat *Transcontinental* from Oregon to New York was a feat in 1925. William Least Heat-Moon's 1995 passage from New York to Oregon, recounted in his 1999 book *River Horse*, was an equal journey of discovery. The annual attempts to set a new speed record on water—as when *Miss America X* exceeded 124 miles per hour in 1933— marked another extreme.

The people and events of maritime history are celebrated in many art forms, including stained glass. This window commemorating maritime explorers was designed by Clement J. Heaton for the living room of financier and yachtsman Arthur Curtiss James. This home, located on the corner of Park Avenue and 69th Street in New York City was built in 1916 and is known to have had a huge cathedral-like living room which included this window. (Mystic Seaport, 59.708)

By the 1930s, as American life required less physical effort, young people looked for ways to test themselves afloat. Some sought out the few fishing and cargo vessels still working under sail and went to sea for the experience. Others sailed off on their own to discover distant corners of the earth. The British mariner, Alan Villiers, provided a sea experience for a few young Americans when he fitted out a former Danish training ship, renamed her *Joseph Conrad*, and began a voyage around the world in 1934. Shortly after, a young American who had tested his own limits at sea, Irving Johnson and his wife Electa, fitted out the schooner *Yankee* to introduce young people to the demands and the adventure of life at sea. For more than 25 years the Johnsons and their several *Yankees* helped young people discover themselves while discovering the world under sail. In the years since, many programs have offered youths and adults the chance to grow through experience on the water, from Mystic Seaport's sail education program to Outward Bound's leadership program.

From the crudest piece of "folk art" to a Winslow Homer seascape, from Herman Melville's *Moby-Dick* to the poetry of Langston Hughes, from Joshua Slocum to today's kayak voyager, the sea inspires creativity. As Melville proclaimed in *Moby-Dick*: "There is magic in it. Let the most absent-minded of men be plunged in his deepest reveries—stand that man on his legs, set his feet a-going, and he will infallibly lead you to water." Where is the magic for you?

AMERICAN MARITIME MUSEUMS

Many American museums contain collections relating to the nation's maritime history. The following 67 members of the Council of American Maritime Museums specialize in the subject and are recommended to readers seeking further information on America's enduring relationship with the sea.

California
Maritime Museum Association of San Diego, North Harbor Drive, San Diego

Maritime Museum of Monterey, Custom House Plaza, Monterey

San Francisco Maritime National Historical Park, San Francisco

Connecticut
Connecticut River Museum, Main Street, Essex

Mystic Seaport, Route 27, Mystic

U.S. Coast Guard Museum, U.S. Coast Guard Academy, Mohegan Avenue, New London

District of Columbia
Navy Museum, Washington Navy Yard

Smithsonian Institution, National Museum of American History

Georgia
Confederate Naval Historical Society, Atlanta

Hawaii
Hawaii Maritime Center, Pier 7, Honolulu

Louisiana
USS *Kidd* & Nautical Center, South River Road, Baton Rouge

Maine
Maine Maritime Museum, Washington Street, Bath

Penobscot Marine Museum, Searsport

Spring Point Museum, Southern Maine Technical College, South Portland

Maryland
Calvert Marine Museum, Solomons

Chesapeake Bay Maritime Museum, St. Michaels

Constellation Foundation, Inc., Pier 1 Pratt Street, Baltimore

Radcliff Maritime Museum, The Maryland Historical Society, West Monument Street, Baltimore

U.S. Naval Academy Museum, U.S. Naval Academy, Annapolis

Massachusetts
Essex Shipbuilding Museum, Main Street, Essex

USS *Constitution*, Boston Naval Shipyard, Boston

USS *Constitution* Museum Foundation, Boston

Hull Lifesaving Museum, Hull

Kendall Whaling Museum, Sharon

M.I.T. Museum, Hart Nautical Collection, Massachusetts Avenue, Cambridge

USS *Massachusetts* Memorial, Battleship Cove, Fall River

Nantucket Historical Association, Nantucket

New Bedford Whaling Museum, Johnny Cake Hill, New Bedford

Peabody Essex Museum, East India Square, Salem

Michigan
Michigan Maritime Museum, South Haven

New Jersey
Barnegat Bay Decoy & Baymen's Museum, Tuckerton

New York
Adirondack Museum, Blue Mountain Lake

American Merchant Marine Museum, U.S. Merchant Marine Academy, Kings Point

Antique Boat Museum, Mary Street, Clayton

Cold Spring Harbor Whaling Museum, Main Street, Cold Spring Harbor

East End Seaport Maritime Museum, Third Street, Greenport

East Hampton Town Marine Museum, Main Street, East Hampton

Erie Canal Museum, Erie Blvd., Syracuse

Hudson River Maritime Museum, Rondout Landing, Kingston

Long Island Maritime Museum,
West Sayville

South Street Seaport Museum,
Front Street, New York

North Carolina
Graveyard of the Atlantic
Museum, Hatteras Village

North Carolina Maritime
Museum,
Front Street, Beaufort

Ohio
Great Lakes Historical Society,
Main Street, Vermilion

Oregon
Columbia River Maritime
Museum,
Marine Drive, Astoria

International Oceanographic
Hero Foundation,
Reedsport

Pennsylvania
Erie Maritime Museum, US Brig
Niagara, State Street, Erie

Independence Seaport Museum,
Penns Landing, Philadelphia

Rhode Island
Herreshoff Marine Museum,
Bristol

Museum of Yachting,
Fort Adams State Park,
Newport

South Carolina
Patriots Point Naval and
Maritime Museum,
Patriots Point, Mt. Pleasant

Texas
Texas Seaport Maritime
Museum,
Strand, Galveston

Vermont
Lake Champlain Maritime
Museum,
Basin Harbor, Vergennes

Virginia
Hampton Roads Naval Museum,
Norfolk

Historic Naval Ships
Association, Virginia Beach

Life-Saving Museum of Virginia,
Virginia Beach

The Mariners' Museum,
Museum Drive, Newport News

Old Coast Guard Station,
Virginia Beach

Portsmouth Naval Shipyard
Museum
High Street, Portsmouth

Reedville Fisherman's Museum,
Reedville

Washington
Anacortes Museum,
Anacortes Center for Wooden
Boats, Valley Street, Seattle

Naval Undersea Museum,
Dowell Street,
Keyport

Northwest Seaport
Valley Street, Seattle

Puget Sound Maritime
Historical Society,
Seattle

Westport Maritime Museum,
Westport

Wisconsin
Wisconsin Maritime Museum,
Maritime Drive, Manitowoc

BECOME A MEMBER TODAY

Mystic Seaport — *The Museum of America and the Sea* — is our country's leading maritime museum, guardian of the largest collections of boats and nautical photography in the world, and champion of the American maritime experience that connects us all. Learn more stories of America and the sea by joining over 25,000 households worldwide and becoming a Mystic Seaport member today. Benefits include free year-round Museum admission; subscriptions to our bimonthly newsletter, the *Wind Rose*, and quarterly magazine, *The Log of Mystic Seaport*; discounts on special member programs and classes, guest admissions, Museum Store purchases and Seamen's Inne dining; and more! Members may also visit our exclusive hospitality lounge in the Membership building; view our Membership Web site, which features the latest program news; sign up for our MemberMail e-mail news bulletin; and purchase Memberwear items, including ties, caps, totebags, and burgees.

FOR FURTHER READING

General

Margaret S. Creighton and Lisa Norling, ed., *Iron Men, Wooden Women: Gender and Seafaring in the Atlantic World, 1700-1920* (Baltimore: Johns Hopkins University Press, 1996)

Luc Cuyvers, *Sea Power: A Global Journey* (Annapolis: Naval Institute Press, 1993)

Benjamin W. Labaree, William M. Fowler, Edward W. Sloan, John B. Hattendorf, Jeffrey J. Safford, and Andrew W. German, *America and the Sea: A Maritime History* (Mystic: Mystic Seaport, 1998)

Walter A. McDougall, *Let the Sea Make a Noise: A History of the North Pacific from Magellan to MacArthur* (New York: Basic Books, 1993)

Peter Neill, *Maritime America: Art and Artifacts from America's Great Nautical Collections* (New York: Balsam Press, 1988)

Coming to America

Peter Morton Coan, *Ellis Island Interviews: In Their Own Words* (New York: Facts on File, 1997)

Dorothy and Thomas Hoobler, *American Family Albums* (New York: Oxford University Press, 1994-97) individual volumes represent different ethnic groups

Ronald Takaki, *A Different Mirror: A History of Multicultural America* (Boston: Little, Brown, 1993)

Hugh Thomas, *The Slave Trade: The Story of the Atlantic Slave Trade: 1440-1870* (New York: Simon and Schuster, 1997)

Following the Rivers

Michael Allen, *Western Rivermen, 1763-1861: Ohio and Mississippi Boatmen and the Myth of the Alligator Horse* (Baton Rouge: Louisiana State University Press, 1990)

Louis C. Hunter, *Steamboats on the Western Rivers: An Economic and Technological History* (reprint, Garden City, New York: Dover, 1994)

David Plowdeon, *End of an Era: The Last of the Great Lakes Steamboats* (New York: W.W. Norton, 1992)

Carol Sheriff, *The Artificial River: The Erie Canal and the Paradox of Progress, 1817-1862* (New York: Hill & Wang, 1996)

Mark Twain, *Life on the Mississippi* (1874)

William Least Heat-Moon, *River Horse: The Logbook of a Boat Across America* (Boston, New York: Houghton Mifflin, 1999)

Connecting America to the World

Parker Bishop Albee, Jr., *Letters from Sea, 1882-1901: Joanna and Lincoln Colcord's Seafaring Childhood* (Gardiner and Searsport, Maine: Tilbury House and Penobscot Marine Museum, 1999)

Richard Henry Dana, Jr., *Two Years Before the Mast* (1841)

Robert Gardiner, ed., *Conway's History of the Ship: Sail's Last Century: The Merchant Sailing Ship 1830-1930* (Annapolis: Naval Institute Press, 1993)

———, *The Shipping Revolution: The Modern Merchant Ship* (Annapolis: Naval Institute Press, 1992)

———, *The Golden Age of Shipping: The Classic Merchant Ship 1900-1960* (Annapolis: Naval Institute Press, 1994)

John McPhee, *Looking for a Ship* (New York: Farrar Straus Giroux, 1990)

Serving at Sea

Tom Clancy, *Submarine: A Guided Tour Inside a Nuclear Warship* (New York: Berkley Books, 1993)

Jean Ebbert and Marie-Beth Hall, *Crossed Currents: Navy Women in a Century of Change* (Washington, D.C.: Brasseys, 1999)

Stephen Howarth, *To Shining Sea: A History of the United States Navy, 1775-1991* (New York: Random House, 1991)

William Marvel, *The Alabama & the Kearsarge: The Sailor's Civil War* (Chapel Hill: University of North Carolina Press, 1996)

Dennis Ringle, *Life in Mr. Lincoln's Navy* (Annapolis: Naval Institute Press, 1998)

Enjoying the Water

Ed Holm, *Yachting's Golden Age, 1880-1905* (New York: Alfred A. Knopf, 1999)

John R. Stilgoe, *Alongshore* (New Haven: Yale University Press, 1994)

Gathering Resources from the Sea

Briton Cooper Busch, *"Whaling Will Never Do for Me": The American Whaleman in the Nineteenth Century* (Lexington: University Press of Kentucky, 1994)

Leslie Leyland Fields, *The Entangling Net: Alaska's Commercial Fishing Women Tell Their Lives* (Urbana: University of Illinois Press, 1997)

John Frye, *The Men All Singing: The Story of Menhaden Fishing* (Virginia Beach: Donning, 1999)

Rudyard Kipling, *Captains Courageous* (1897)

Herman Melville, *Moby-Dick* (1851)

Finding Inspiration

Horace Beck, *Folklore and the Sea* (Mystic: Mystic Seaport Museum, 1996)

Stan Hugill, *Shanties from the Seven Seas* (Mystic: Mystic Seaport Museum, 1994)

Haskell Springer, ed., *America and the Sea: A Literary History* (Athens: University of Georgia Press, 1995)

John Wilmerding, *American Marine Painting* (New York: Harry N. Abrams, 1987)

INDEX

(Includes text and picture captions)